SPACE,
ATOMS,
AND GOD

SPACE,
ATOMS,
AND GOD

*Christian Faith and
the Nuclear-space Age*

By Jack Finegan

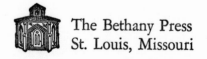

The Bethany Press
St. Louis, Missouri

Copyright © 1959

BY

The Bethany Press

PREFACE

This book has to do with the new age which began when the first atom bombs were exploded and when the first Sputniks began to circle the earth, but it has more to do with the new age which began when Jesus Christ came preaching the good news of the kingdom of God. The first section of the book describes our new epoch of atomic power and space travel, and considers some of its implications in regard to the Christian faith. The second section has to do with the biblical understanding of the old age and the new age, and where it is that we presently stand in relation to both. The third section asks about the nature of God and the connection with him of the world of atoms and of space. The fourth section speaks of the ethical task of the Christian who lives in the world that now is but looks toward the world that is yet to be. With such as its scope it is hoped that the book will provide some stimulus to and guidance in Christian thought in the age of atomic power and space travel.

Since man is now going "up" into space and utilizing the "atom," I wanted to call this book *Up and Atom*, but the publishers disapproved of this frivolity and so the volume is issued now under the more restrained title, *Space, Atoms, and God*.

JACK FINEGAN

University Christian Church
Pacific School of Religion
Berkeley, California

CONTENTS

PART ONE:

The Age We Live In

CHAPTER I

The Ends of the Ages

In 1 Corinthians 10:11 Paul speaks, in the literal rendering of the American Standard Version, of those "upon whom the ends of the ages are come." According to this statement, those whom he addressed and, therefore, we too, are living at the ends of the ages.

The idea of "ages," which Paul uses, is familiar to us. The word "age" is literally *aeon*. It means a period of time, usually a long period of time, and usually also a period of time marked by a distinctive character. About which ages Paul was speaking, he does not explicitly tell us in this text. We know that he was a Jew and the Jewish people commonly spoke of this age and the age that is to come, of the age that is now and the age that is to be. Paul may have had that in mind. However, he was writing in Greek and working among the Greeks and we know that the Greeks thought of a number of successive periods of time. As we learn from Hesiod, the Greeks spoke of a Golden Age which existed long ago in the past in which man was free from infirmity and enjoyed perfect happiness. After that came a Silver Age which was characterized by luxury and pride,

11

then a Bronze Age marked by violence and war. Finally
there was an Iron Age in which a degenerate mankind bore
the burden of toil and selfishness, and Hesiod believed that
he was living in that age. Thus Paul might conceivably
have been thinking of a succession of ages after the Greek
pattern.

As for ourselves, we customarily think along the latter
line and divide our history upon earth into a series of ages.
The divisions we usually employ are those of the Stone Age,
the Copper and Stone Age, the Bronze Age, and the Iron
Age. At any rate, we are familiar with the idea of successive
and distinctive periods in the history of man.

The Marks of Our Age

Paul is speaking not only about ages but also about the
ends of the ages, so we must ask what the word "end"
means. In the Greek language in which Paul is writing this
word has several connotations. For one thing it means "last."
Therefore Paul must be saying that we are living in the last
part or last parts of the ages. Now what has happened
within our very day gives us a fresh sense that Paul may be
right and that we may actually be living now in the last part
or one of the last parts of the ages. The first age, according
to our usual manner of reckoning, was the Stone Age. As
the artifacts which have been found show, man at that
time picked up stones and used them for implements and
weapons, gradually learning how to chip the sides to make
better cutting edges. This age may have begun, it is believed, a million years ago. In the Copper and Stone Age
which, at least in the Near East, began about 4500 B.C. man
began to use copper as well as stone. When he learned to
alloy the copper with tin or other elements and thus make
it harder and more useful, the Bronze Age began. This was
around 3000 B.C. About 1200 B.C. the Iron Age began. From

then until our very day, iron and steel have been the materials most characteristically employed.

It is obvious that this way of dividing the ages marks the successive periods of time by the materials most typically used in them. But we know well that all of these materials —stone, copper, bronze, and iron—are themselves made up of something more fundamental which we call the atoms. The remarkable thing which has happened in our time is that man has begun to use the atoms themselves, the fundamental stuff out of which all materials are made. This assuredly marks the inauguration of a new age and, since it is characterized by the utilization of the very "building blocks" out of which all other things are made, it would seem to be properly recognized as the "last" of the ages.

Likewise, the fact that man has now begun to go into space seems also to be a step of an ultimate or "last" character. Man now uses the atom, man now begins to go up into space, and the two things belong together, for it is atomic power which will presumably provide the most effective energy for space travel. How long this age may continue is, of course, not thereby indicated. The Stone Age endured for half a million years, some of the other ages of which we have spoken lasted for a few thousand. The new age might be brief or almost inconceivably long. In any event it seems to have a character of "lastness" about it.

The word "end" also means "goal." In Greek it is *telos,* and this root may be recognized in our word "teleology" which we use to describe that which is directed toward a purposed outcome. In this connotation, too, we have a sense of living at the ends of the ages, for in our time the goals of which men have dreamed for thousands of years have been reached. The use of the atom and the penetration of space have both been the object of men's thought and hope for a long time. Speaking here of the atom and leaving further consideration of space for the next chapter, we remember that the idea of the atom was conceived of as anciently as by the Greeks. Democritus, born in the fifth century B.C., believed that matter was made up of countless particles moving in empty space and colliding endlessly with one another. Thus they came, he thought, to form aggregates of considerable size, density, and weight, which differed in being hard or soft, smooth or rough, sweet or bitter, and of one color or another. Since these particles were thought of as the ultimate units of everything, the Greeks called them *atomos,* which means uncut or incapable of being divided, and as late as thirty or forty years ago standard textbooks were still speaking of the atom as the smallest and indivisible particle of the universe.

Meanwhile, however, the idea also arose that it might be possible to transmute the elements. This was the dream of the alchemists. Writing on "The Origin of Alchemy," R. J. Forbes[1] shows that alchemy began in Babylonia and in Egypt in the pre-Christian centuries. It was strong in Alexandria in the early Christian centuries. From the East the idea was carried by the Arabs to Western Europe where it was prominent at the end of the Middle Ages. It was the hope of the alchemists that base metals might be changed into precious ones, lead for example into silver or into gold. With Paracelsus it was also the hope that medicines could be made which would be wonderfully effective. Now in our time the dream of the centuries has come to pass. The once indivisible atom has been found to be divisible and, when it is divided and its component parts are rearranged, different and even new elements are made and prodigious powers are released.

As commonly presented for us laymen, the picture of the

[1] *Studies in Ancient Technology.* (Leiden: E. J. Brill, 1955), pp. 121-144.

atomic world is something like this. The hydrogen atom
contains one proton with a positive electric charge and one
electron with a negative electric charge. Since an atom is so
small that twenty-five trillion of them could lie side by side
in an inch, we need a larger scale model by which to visual-
ize it. Let the proton of the hydrogen atom be a ten-inch
toy balloon at the center of a circle ten miles in diameter.
On the circumference of the circle the electron is a small
marble whirling around at 1350 miles per second. Now step
by step we add one more proton and one more electron up
to ninety-two, as well as some neutrons and no one knows
yet how many other minor charges, and we have uranium.
Here, then, we are indeed dealing with the very building
blocks of the universe and by the process of addition or sub-
traction the transmutation of the elements, the dream of
the alchemists, is possible. To turn lead into gold we have
only to remove from the lead atom three protons and elec-
trons and eight neutrons. The cost of the procedure is, of
course, about $1,000,000 an ounce, nevertheless transmuta-
tion of the elements may now be said to be an everyday
occurrence. Furthermore, as we know well, with the fission
of the uranium atom and the fusion of the hydrogen atom
tremendous power is released. So with the use of the atom
as with man's reaching into space, goals of the ages have
been attained in our time and, in this sense, we are living
at the ends of the ages.

The word "end" also means "revenue." In Greek it is the
same word which was used for tax, custom, or duty. Accordingly A. Souter has translated our text, "the (spiritual)
revenues of the ages." Indeed the revenues of the ages are
come upon us. We receive the benefits of the labors of the
years. In 1957 the Vallecitos Atomic Power Plant in Pleas-
anton, California, was turned on and the people of the
nearby Bay Area, including the city of Berkeley, began

using atomic electricity, the first time in history that atomic electricity was produced commercially in a privately financed plant. Likewise, in the latter city in a hospital wing related to the Radiation Laboratory of the University of California, I have visited patients upon whom for the first time direct atomic radiation was being used in an assault upon one of the most stubborn of man's diseases. The beneficial revenues of the ages are becoming available to us.

But the word "end" also means "termination." It can signify cessation and finish. This is the uneasy feeling which haunts us as we read Paul's statement and contemplate what has transpired in our time. Is it the close of civilization which is at hand?

Our Age Still Part of the Old Age

We live at a time when almost unbelievable goals have been achieved and great revenues are ours, yet when uneasy apprehension of possibly imminent doom also hangs over us. We live at a climactic time in the succession of the ages, yet one which may also be catastrophic and concluding. The very fact that the attainment in our time of the dreams of the centuries thus brings us fear as well as hope, and threatens us with suffering as well as promises us joy, shows that this wonderful new age in which we live is in reality still a part of the old age. If we think of a succession of numerous periods in human history, our period has a character of climax about it. But if we think of just two periods all together, an old age of human contradiction and sin and a new age of real blessedness, our time has to be considered still a part of the old age.

The atomic age began, it is customary to say, on August 6, 1945. What is the significance of that date? It is the date when we dropped the first atomic bomb on Hiroshima,

Japan, and at a single stroke killed or incapacitated over half the inhabitants of an entire city. Out of a population of 255,000, 64,000 died, 72,000 were burned or maimed. If that was the launching of the age of the atom then the age of the atom is still a part of the old age in which is much that is grim and terrible. As Carl Sandburg has phrased it, the record of human progress now includes

the fights of man from club and sling to the pink mushroom of Hiroshima.[2]

When the hydrogen bomb was tested at a Pacific island, Francis Brennan wrote this "Prayer at Eniwetok":

O Lord
Guide us now
We have measured counted
    weighed
And the search is almost
                                        done.
Within the
                    glass and metal
Calculators
The myriad correlations end
And we are assembled
To verify
The terminal
                                        Fact.

O Lord
Help us now
We see Space as Time
Light as Matter
Matter as
                                        Force.

[2] Quoted in *The Pulpit*, Dec. 1957, p. 3.

Enveloped in the
Surging
Flame-Storms
Of a thousand

               suns

We know too
One is all
And all is

               One.

Thus we came
Upon Revelation's

               Image.

O Lord
Deliver us now
We press close on Your
   domain:
We beheld in

               Fission

The searing flashes
Of the wrathful ancient gods;
Now in

               Fusion

We do release
The second half
of aeon-locked finality:

          Regeneration.

O Lord
Grant us now
The last Great Reason.
We tremble in discovery
For slowly comes the deadly
             Question:

Is this not the
Power
That giveth and the
Power
That taketh away?

Amen.[3]

Likewise the space age, the inauguration of which on
October 4, 1957, will be described more fully in the next
chapter, brought the world quite as much fear as hope. As
the first artificial satellite was launched, Theodore A. Gill
wrote: "Is not this new seal of our grandeur also a sign of
our shame? Where are the glad songs that everyone ought
to be able to sing before such a miracle wrought so won-
drously by that miracle, man? Where is the single, world-
wide exhilaration and exaltation there ought to be for this
elevation of our ceiling, this vast sweeping back of our
horizons? Has a single man's glorying in the achievement
been untouched by dread? Does it not say something about
us that at our greatest we must fear that greatness most
greatly?"[4]

The New Age

These are the marks of the fact that our truly wonderful
new age, the nuclear-space age, is still, in spite of all its
glory, a part of the old age in which the grandeur of man is
strangely mingled with his misery.[5] But at the same time we
may declare that the new age, the really new age, the age

[3] *The Saturday Review,* Dec. 13, 1952, p. 34. Used by permission.
[4] *The Pulpit,* Dec. 1957, p. 3. Copyrighted by the Christian Century
Foundation and reprinted by permission of *The Pulpit* from the issue
of December, 1957.
[5] cf. the title of the book by David E. Roberts, *The Grandeur and
Misery of Man* (New York: Oxford University Press, 1955).

which we desperately need, has also already begun. It is not certain in the statement we have been studying whether the Apostle Paul was thinking that there is a whole succession of ages as the Greeks believed, or just two ages, the old and the new, as the Jews thought. It does seem plain from all his writing that he did believe that the new age had already begun. Indeed the fact that he speaks literally in the plural of "the *ends* of the ages," has been explained by Johannes Weiss as meaning that the end-point of the old age and the beginning-point of the new age had come together in Paul's day. Concerning this view of the times we will say more later in this book. Here let us simply affirm the faith taught by Paul and the whole New Testament, that with Jesus Christ the new age has begun.

One way of putting it is to say that that new age began when he showed the power of love in his own life. Observing that this is something as simple as taking a child upon one's knee and seeing in it the kingdom of God, or giving a cup of cold water, or meeting curses with prayers, and that such things seem almost inconsequential alongside Oak Ridge, Argonne Laboratory, and Yucca Flats, Harold A. Bosley remarks, "*A nation can possess all of the celebrated 'know-how' in the world, but if it has not love, it is nothing!*"[6] In a well-known mural on Rockefeller Center in New York City, humanity is seen looking toward Christ, and the accompanying inscription expresses the thought with which we may appropriately conclude this chapter: "Man's ultimate destiny depends not on whether he can learn new lessons or make new discoveries and conquests, but on his acceptance of the lessons taught him close upon two thousand years ago."

[6] *The Christian-Evangelist,* Dec. 16, 1957, p. 1522. Used by permission.

CHAPTER 2

Theology and Space

The achievements of recent time have begun a new age, the nuclear-space age, yet the ambiguities of this age in which we experience at least as much fear as hope show that this is actually still a part of the old age. Accordingly what we need very much and indeed need more than ever is the really new age which was begun by Jesus Christ. This we said in the preceding chapter with special reference to the fact that in our age man has unloosed the power of the atom. Now we must work out essentially the same analysis with regard more particularly to the other chief new fact, namely that man has begun to go into space.

The Space Age

The fact that man has now taken the first steps toward going out into the space which surrounds his planet marks the beginning of a remarkable and climactic period in the divisions of human history. In the preceding chapter we saw that the history of man may be divided according to the materials most characteristically used in successive periods and that his present utilization of the fundamental stuff out of which all the various materials are made, namely the atoms, marks a distinctive, long-sought, and also ominous period. Now we may note another way in which the history of man may be divided. This is according to where, in successive periods, he lives and where he goes. By his natural endowment man goes on the land. He has legs and feet and they are better adapted for walking over the earth than for anything else although, to be sure, in our time there seems to be some danger that man will forget how to walk and allow his pedal extremities to atrophy because he has so many automobiles and other conveyances in which to ride wherever he goes. Nevertheless, by natural endowment man is a creature of the land. He does not have gills to breathe under water; he does not have his own wings with which to fly in the air. He belongs first of all upon the solid earth and his first age of history is the land age.

It was therefore an achievement and it marked a new age when man began to go upon the water. Like most things, it may be supposed that this began little by little. Perhaps someone caught a floating log and drifted down a stream on it. By around 1200 B.C. Egyptian monuments contain records of a people of the sea who were pressing in upon Egypt, and in a temple of Ramses III at Medinet Habu there is the earliest known representation of a salt-water naval battle in a great relief carving. Soon the Phoenicians were launching out upon the Mediterranean on trading expeditions which carried them all the way to what we know as Spain. Later in the Pacific the Polynesians developed a remarkable art of navigation. Within our own memory, "Britannia rules the waves" was a proud slogan and control of the seas meant control everywhere. This was the age of man which was marked out by his going upon the waters.

It was a further achievement and the making of a new age when man began to go into the air. The air is also an ocean of a sort, but different in that it is almost intangible and invisible. Yet you can move your hand fast enough to feel the pressure of the air against it, you can gulp the air into your lungs, and in some places badly beset by smog you can even see what you are breathing at the same time! So at last man went into the air. In 1903 the Wright brothers flew a heavier-than-air machine. They went so short a distance that today the wingspread of a B-36 is greater than the length of their first flight. They went so slowly that they barely kept aloft. Man, however, was actually in the air. Today, little more than fifty years later, machines recognizably related to that first one of the Wright brothers have gone very high and very fast, so high that a major portion of the atmosphere is beneath, so fast that multiples of the velocity of sound must be used to measure the speed. Thus the Bell X-2 research aircraft has gone to 126,000 feet, which is high in the stratosphere where perhaps 97 per cent of the atmosphere is beneath, and has traveled over 2,100 miles per hour, which is approximately three times the speed of sound. And in recent time control of the air has meant supremacy upon earth.

Once again now it is a further accomplishment, one of incalculable promise and one that marks the beginning of a new period, that man has taken the initial steps toward going into space. The atmosphere of which we have been speaking extends up to no one knows exactly how far, but to a limited distance. The lowest part is called the "troposphere" and extends upward seven or eight miles. Measured by weight, about three-fourths of the air is here. Air, almost intangible though it is, does have weight and at sea level it presses upon us with a force of 14.7 pounds per square inch. Above the troposphere is the stratosphere, which we have already mentioned, which extends on up to fifty or sixty miles. Here the air is too thin to support life and man must carry oxygen and artificial pressure with him. Above that is the ionosphere which may go on up to five hundred miles or so. This is the electrified region which reflects back our radio signals. Finally there is the exosphere where there are only a few molecules of matter. How far that region extends no one knows, but it may be to a distance of a thousand miles or more. Beyond that, wherever it does come to an end, is the black nothingness of space.

Man has dreamed of going up there for a long time. In earlier days there may not have been such a distinction made between the atmosphere and space as we have just indicated, but at any event man wished to go as far up and as near to the heavenly bodies which he saw overhead as he could. Persian legends contain a record about a certain king, Kai Kaus, who must have lived as early as 1000 B.C., who "went to the sky." The machine in which he made the memorable ascent was a square box. On each corner of the box a spear was fixed with the point up. On the points of the spears were chunks of meat. Tethered to the box were four great eagles on cords which would not quite allow them to reach the meat above their heads. As they flapped their wings, straining upward for the meat, they lifted the entire contraption and King Kai Kaus went to the sky. The Greeks told about Icarus, for whom his father made wings. Rashly the young man flew too near the sun, the wax in the wings melted, and he plummeted into the sea.

Men have done preliminary things which have prepared the way for going into space, whether that purpose was consciously in view or not. Around A.D. 1200 the Chinese were warring with the Tartars. With the intention of making a bomb they put a chemical mixture, an early form of gunpowder, into a cylinder which was sealed at one end and open at the other. When lighted, the mixture instead of exploding burned fiercely and the flames rushed out of the open end. The cylinder was projected into the air. When a stick was fixed to the side, more stability was given. Then the strange new weapons were fired toward the enemy, and so the first rockets were in use. Although we may not recall the full significance of the matter when we sing the song, there is a phrase about "the rocket's red glare" in our own national anthem, and this is because the British used rockets against the Americans in the War of 1812. The American inventor, Robert Goddard, pioneered purposefully in the field of rocket propulsion and in 1923 sent aloft successfully the first liquid fuel rocket.

Finally in our own day, on October 4 and November 3, 1957, the first two man-made satellites were put into orbits around the earth. The first satellite reportedly weighed 184 pounds and went out in its elliptical orbit to 560 miles from the earth, the second weighed over 1,100 pounds and went out to 937 miles. In Russian the letter S means "with," the word *put* means "way" or "path," and *nik* is the ending for a noun and has a diminutive sense, hence that which goes with on the path is a Sputnik, a traveling companion, a satellite. Out there where the Sputniks have been orbiting is the edge of space. Presumably the reports sent back by the Russian and later the American satellites, the first of which, the "Explorer," was put into its orbit on January 31, 1958, will help us know more exactly where that edge is, but to the best of our present knowledge we may say that man-made objects have now been sent at least as far as to the beginnings of that new frontier and that last frontier, the realm of space itself. Furthermore, the reported velocity of the Sputniks of 18,000 miles per hour needs to be increased but comparatively little more to 25,000 miles per hour to provide the theoretical velocity for escape from the earth's field of gravitation and to send an object on its way into further space. Man has therefore in our very day taken the dramatic first step toward going into space. To have

stood in the predawn earth darkness and have watched
Sputnik I's rocket and Sputnik II come over, each a tiny
moon of light passing in steady speed in three or four
minutes from horizon to horizon on a journey circling the
globe in ninety minutes, is to have seen something which
at least to one observer was more exciting than it would
have been to see Columbus land, and is to have witnessed
the opening of an epoch of more incalculable possibilities
than any previous one ever in the material history of man.

Theology Has Something To Do With Space

It is interesting to remember, next, that theology has had
something to do with man's looking into space. A dream of
the years which has previously appeared to most people
like utter fantasy has now begun to be a practical reality.
Back of this practical accomplishment lies theoretical knowledge. Newton's third law of motion, for example, is involved. Isaac Newton, who lived around 1700, was the man
who watched apples fall from trees and wondered why they
always fell in the same direction. Why did they always
fall down, why did they not sometimes fall up? He noticed
that things are in motion and he wondered why this is so
since, he felt, they would hardly move of their own accord.
Finally he formulated three laws of motion, the third of
which says: "For every action there is an opposite and equal
reaction." You step from a rowboat to the dock and the
force which pushes you toward the dock pushes the boat
away from the dock; if you do not allow for this, you may
fall in the water between. You shoot a gun and the force
which propels the bullet forward is felt equally although
over a wider area in the recoil of the gun against your
shoulder. The law just stated describes the principle of all
rocket propulsion, and this theoretical knowledge is necessary to the practical use of rockets.

Back of the theoretical knowledge there had to be observation. Newton watched the apples fall from the tree, and he and other people, the watchers of the sky through the centuries, scanned the heavens and looked at all the dots of light which are there. Out of these observations comes to us the science of astronomy, a science which once may have seemed remote from immediate concerns but which now seems of crucial importance for survival itself.

Much of this observation has undoubtedly been purely scientific in character and has grown out of what we would call purely scientific interest. Yet it is also a fact that at least in the beginning the scientific interest was often mingled with what we would call theological interest. At an early time men thought that the points of light in the sky were heavenly beings. The gleaming planet in the evening sky is Venus; the one that glares more malevolently in reddish light is Mars. These were the names of deities in the ancient world. The lights were the deities, or their homes. When we come across the great watershed which separates all other ancient thinking from the knowledge which is found in the Bible, and stand among the people of Israel to whom it was given to hear the word of the one true God, there is no longer any confusion between God and the things which he has made. Yet precisely because the things which are made are the handiwork of the great Creator, the writers of the Bible look toward them with reverent and attentive interest. As they contemplate what is made, they think of the Maker, and so they find that the heavens are telling the glory of God;

> and the firmament proclaims his handiwork.—
> Psalm 19:1

So in ancient times the priests were sometimes astronomers, the temples were sometimes observatories, and the

Sanhedrin at Jerusalem had as part of its duties astronomical observations and calculations. Of the Jewish rabbi, Mar Samuel, who lived in Babylonia around A.D. 200 and directed the school at Nehardea, it was said that he was as familiar with the paths of heaven as with the streets of his own city. Theology has had something to do with man's looking into space.

Space Leads to Theology

Now in our time man's looking into space and his projected going into space ought to lead him to return to theology. Man in space will still be a human being. Some things will change for him out in space. In orbital or in space flight, for example, man will be weightless. This will pose new problems. If you try to pour out some water, it will just float in the air. If you sneeze accidentally, you may propel yourself roughly against the wall. Man will have to adjust to certain changes out in space, yet essentially he will still be just like what he is here upon earth. He will still have his hopes and his fears, his temptations and his trials, and his greatest problem will still be himself and his second greatest problem his relation to other people. He will still have his sorrows and his griefs. Man will still be a human being, and will still need God just as much as ever. In the editorial columns of *The New York Times* this remarkable statement appeared only a few days after the launching of the first Sputnik:

The creature who descended from a tree or crawled out of a cave a few thousand years ago is now on the eve of incredible journeys. Yet it is not these journeys that chiefly matter. Will we be happier for seeing the other side of the moon or strolling among the Martian meadows of asphodel?

The truth is at once more ominous, more exacting and more enchanting. The greatest adventure of all is not to go to the moon or to explore the rings of Saturn. It is, rather, to understand the heart and soul of man and to turn away from wrath and destruction and toward creativeness and brotherly love.[1]

Man in space will still also be a creature and not the Creator. At this point man is always in danger of forgetting his real status. Periodically, when his achievement is great, he becomes proud of his accomplishment and forgets who he really is, and from the time of the tower of Babel until now, confusion results. It is reported that the Russian magazine *Krokodil* carried this arrogant verse:

> *And here we have our Sputnik*
> *No secret: the newborn planet*
> *Is modest about its size,*
> *But this symbol of intellect and light*
> *Is made by us, and not by the God*
> *Of the Old Testament.*[2]

Similarly one thinks of the majestic paraphrase of Psalm 19 by Joseph Addison in which the heavenly bodies sing, "The hand that made us is divine," and imagines that now a new version may emerge in which the satellites declare, "The hand that made us is human."

True as it is that the satellites are made by man, it is also true that in order to make them man has had to learn and conform to some of the laws of a marvelous and mysterious universe. God is so great that he allows all men to use the laws of his world whether or not they recognize that this is his world, and whether or not they stop to be grateful to him. But in all we do, we are simply making use of what is already here and what no man could of himself bring into being. Some indeed will surely be moved to greater awe and reverence as they are privileged to look upon more of the marvels and mysteries of space. Thus in

[1] *The New York Times,* Oct. 7, 1957, p. 26-C. Used by permission.
[2] *Time,* Nov. 18, 1957, p. 67. Used by permission.

1957 Major David G. Simons soared in a balloon to an altitude of 102,000 feet where 99 per cent of the earth's atmosphere was beneath him, and came back from his extended sojourn at that great height to describe the sunset and the sunrise which he witnessed through "'the pristine clarity of the edge of space" as something of such beauty that it was almost impossible to communicate it fully. In space man will still be creature and not Creator, and the beauty and mystery and marvel of God's world will be all about him.

Yet again, man in space is man in danger and in peril. With every human achievement comes corresponding imperilment. The greater the achievement the greater the imperilment. Indeed it seems easier to set loose the destructive than to accomplish the constructive. The atom bomb was released before atomic power was used for peaceful ends. Jet aircraft have flown a great deal for military purposes before they have flown much for commercial usages. We have to work harder to harness great forces for good than to set them free in the first place. Therefore we need the guidance of God. In the year 1957 which saw the opening of the space age President Eisenhower said truly:

The world now has a choice between the technology of abundance and the technology of destruction, between the use of power for constructive purposes or for war and desolation. And as we contemplate this simple truth, I think we are moved to gain the deeper conviction that no matter how long or how far scientists may go in probing the secrets of nature for the benefit of man, yet it will be only the Master Scientist, only the Almighty, who will delve deeply enough into the hearts and minds of men to lead us to use these great secrets properly, to develop in us the compassion, sympathy, the understanding, the consideration for other points of view that will eventually bring peace —a just peace—to the world.

That is why the age of space must lead us to return to theology and to the God of whom theology speaks.

CHAPTER 3

Christ Amidst the Planets

Thus far we have described the beginning in our time of the nuclear-space age, a dramatically new period in the history of man. We have recognized that the combination of hope and fear which it entails shows that it is still a part of the old age and that we need the truly new age of God about which Jesus Christ tells us and which has indeed already begun. When we think of the work which Christ has done to begin the kingdom of God, we now have to ask about the significance of that work in relation to the vaster spaces of which man has recently become more aware.

Man knows more now about the planets than formerly. Even ancient man noticed the planets. If you look at the sky at night, you will see innumerable twinkling lights up there. Those are the stars. There are also some lights which shine steadily and are noticeable among the others on that account. They are the planets. The stars are of course in motion but since they are so immensely far from us they appear to stay in the same position in relation to one another. The steadily gleaming lights which are the planets, however, move against the background of the stars. This also attracted attention to them at an early time, and led

31

the Greeks to call them *planētēs,* which means "wanderers." Not only the Greeks but also the Egyptians and the Babylonians before them were familiar with the planets. Since they thought that the earth was the center and that both the sun and the moon as well as the other bodies went around it, they counted together the sun and moon and the five planets which are readily visible to the unaided eye, namely, Mercury, Venus, Mars, Jupiter, and Saturn, and considered that there were seven planets all together. In 1543, the year Copernicus died, publication of the work of this astronomer made it evident that the sun is actually the center of the system and the earth itself is just one of the planets revolving about the sun. By 1619 Johannes Kepler had formulated three mathematical laws to describe the orbits of the planets which were found to be not strictly circles. With the telescope, which was developed as an astronomical instrument by Galileo in 1609, more planets were seen: in 1781 Uranus; in 1801 Ceres, the first of a large number of minor planets known as planetoids or asteroids; in 1846 Neptune; and in 1930, on a photographic plate, Pluto. Thus we now consider that the sun is at the center of the system and that there revolve around it Mercury, Venus, the Earth, Mars, the asteroids, Jupiter, Saturn, Uranus, Neptune, and Pluto.

We also think now that it may become possible to travel to the planets. Rocket power is prodigiously effective. It is commonly measured in thrust pounds. A thrust pound is approximately equal to one horsepower at a speed of 370 miles per hour. As the speed increases, however, the horsepower equivalent multiplies out of all proportion. Thus the liquid-fuel rocket motor of the high-altitude research vehicle known as the Martin Viking is rated around 21,000 pounds of thrust, but by the time it reaches a speed of 4,500 miles per hour the energy expenditure is equal to some 230,000 horsepower. Compared with this, Sputnik I is believed to have been launched with an initial thrust of 250,000-300,000 pounds, and Sputnik II with 800,000 to 1,000,000 pounds. With this power an orbital velocity of 18,000 miles per hour has been attained by the satellites and this, as we have noted, needs only to be increased to 25,000 miles per hour to provide escape from the gravitational field of the earth. If we may then proceed on our way in space at this speed, travel over great distances becomes possible. The moon is about 240,000 miles from the earth. At 25,000 miles per hour it should be reached in under ten hours. The distance is only ten times the circumference of the earth, and from October to the end of December, 1957, the first Sputnik was reported to have circled the earth about 1,300 times, thus going immensely farther than the distance to the moon. From the moon, with its lesser gravitational attraction, a fresh start should be readily possible and at the continued speed of 25,000 miles per hour one would come within a reasonable length of time to some of the planets. The planet traveling in an orbit next inside the orbit of the earth and nearer the sun is Venus. At its closest point it comes within 25,000,000 miles of the earth. It should, therefore, be reached in 1,000 hours. The planet traveling in an orbit just outside that of the earth is Mars. It comes to within 35,000,000 miles, and Sputnik I traveled that far before it disintegrated.

The amazing possibility which has been the fantasy of man's earlier imaginings thus appears to be coming reasonably into sight. Man may travel to the planets. Indeed Dr. Wernher von Braun, famed expert in this field, declared in 1957 that by 2057 trips to the moon will be commonplace, expeditions will be made to Mars and Venus, and exploration will be under way on Saturn, Jupiter, and their satellites. If rockets approaching the speed of light—186,000 miles per second—should be developed, as Professor Cyrill Stanyukovich of the Soviet Academy of Sciences is reported to have predicted, then it might be possible to go on into outer space beyond the solar system itself. The other stars themselves might come within reach, for the nearest one is only about four and one-third light-years away. Writing on this subject, Charles Coombs says there are some who think such journeys may become possible, fantastic though the idea must seem at present. "Yet who is to say," he asks, "whether it is fantasy—or destiny!"[1]

It is furthermore believed now that there may be many more planets than we used to suppose. Around our sun revolve the planets of which we have been speaking. In many cases their own natural satellites revolve around these planets. Thus the moon revolves about the earth and, as far as we know, only Mercury, Venus, and Pluto are not attended by such companions. Since this seems to be the natural arrangement of astronomical bodies, it seemes likely that it also prevails in other places than here. According to one catalogue there are 40,000 stars more or less like our sun within our immediate neighborhood. In our explorable universe there are stars to the number of ten to the twentieth power. If there are one hundred million million million sources of light and warmth like our sun, it seems unlikely that ours would be the only one which is accompanied by planets. Indeed Harlow Shapley, director until 1952 of the Harvard Observatory, declares flatly: "Millions of planetary systems must exist."[2]

If there are so many planets, and since there is life on this one which we know, it seems that there may be life

[1] Charles Coombs, *Rockets, Missiles, and Moons* (New York: William Morrow and Company, 1957), p. 243. Used by permission.

[2] Harlow Shapley, "Man's Fourth Adjustment," in *The American Scholar*, Vol. 25, No. 4, Autumn 1956, p. 456. Used by permission of Harlow Shapley.

elsewhere too. The planet Venus is much like the earth in size, mass, and density, and its surface appears to be covered with clouds or vapor. Mars is smaller and cooler than the earth. Observed closely, there are white spots at the poles and masses of gray-green around the equator. These seem to change with the seasons, and could be ice and vegetation respectively. If there is plant life, there could also be animal life. Percival Lowell, founder of the Flagstaff Observatory, even thought that he could see fine markings on Mars, commonly called canals, which he believed were the work of intelligent beings. In the universe at large, if there are as many planetary systems as just suggested, then it seems unlikely that there should not be life in some of them. If life has evolved there under conditions somewhat like those here, it might be life somewhat like what we know; if in some places it has evolved over a much longer period of time than here, it might be on higher levels than we know.

In an article in *The American Scholar* from which we have already quoted his estimate that millions of planetary systems must exist, Harlow Shapley raises this question in these words:

On some of these planets is there actually life; or is that biochemical operation strangely limited to our planet, No. 3 in the family of the sun, which is a run-of-the-mill star located in the outer part of a galaxy that contains a hundred thousand million other stars—and this galaxy but one of millions already on the records? Is life thus restricted?

To this he answers flatly:

Of course not. We are not alone. . . . To put it briefly: biochemistry and microbiology, with the assistance of geophysics, astronomy and other sciences, have gone so far in bridging the gap between the inanimate and the living that we can no longer doubt but that whenever the physics, chemistry and climates are right on a planet's surface, life will emerge and persist.

That man must now bring his thinking into line with the possibility and probability just stated Shapley calls the necessary "fourth adjustment" in human thinking. Beginning with his thoughts presumably centered on himself, man had first to make the geocentric adjustment and learn to think of the earth. After that he had to adjust to the heliocentric concept, that the solar system is centered on the sun rather than on the earth. Then he had to realize that the sun is only one star near the edge of a great galaxy of stars, and this galaxy only one among a multitude of galaxies, thus he had to envision a galactocentric universe. Now, in a fourth major adjustment, man must reckon with the fact that he may not be alone as an intelligent creature in the universe. "In conclusion," writes the astronomer, "I need not emphasize the possible relevance to philosophy and perhaps to religion of this fourth adjustment in man's view of himself in the material universe."[3]

The God of Everything

It is a necessary task in our time, therefore, to ask about the meaning of the work of Christ in the light of the planetary dimensions of present-day thought. For one thing, in considering this matter, we may affirm that the God whom Jesus Christ revealed is the God of everything. When we contemplate the vast universe of which we have just been speaking, we can scarcely fail to find it marvelous and mysterious. In his book, *The Nature of the Universe,* Fred Hoyle, fellow of Saint John's College at Cambridge, rejects what he understands to be the outlook of Christianity but rejects the viewpoint of materialism as well and writes these remarkable words:

When by patient inquiry we learn the answer to any problem, we always find, both as a whole and in detail, that the answer thus

[3] *Ibid.*, pp. 456-457.

revealed is finer in concept and design than anything we could ever have arrived at by a random guess. And this, I believe, will be the same for the deeper issues we have just been discussing. I think that all our present guesses are likely to prove but a very pale shadow of the real thing; and it is on this note that I must now finish. Perhaps the most majestic feature of our whole existence is that while our intelligences are powerful enough to penetrate deeply into the evolution of this quite incredible Universe, we still have not the smallest clue to our own fate.[4]

When the universe makes such an impression of transcendent mystery upon the inquiring mind, it seems not unreasonable to advance to the thought of it all as the handiwork of an infinite God. Writing on *The Origin of the Earth,* W. M. Smart, professor of astronomy in the University of Glasgow, says:

When we study the Universe and appreciate its grandeur and orderliness, it seems to me that we are led to the recognition of a Creative Power and Cosmic Purpose that transcends all that our limited minds can comprehend. . . . To one astronomer at least "The Heavens are telling the Glory of God and the Wonder of His Works."[5]

This far man may reasonably come, it seems, by his own observation and meditation. Then he reads the Bible and studies the teachings of Jesus, and finds here an assurance and a revelation of God as indeed the One from whom are all things. Jesus speaks of the Father with the perfect confidence of his own personal knowledge and says, for a single example, this amazing thing: "Are not two sparrows sold for a penny? And not one of them will fall to the ground without your Father's will. But even the hairs of your head are all numbered." (Matthew 10:29-30.) There were in 1957 about 2.7 billion people on this planet, and God has numbered the hairs of their heads! It is not more remarkable than that that he should know all the millions of planetary systems of which we have been speaking. Of

[4] New York: Harper & Brothers, 1950, p. 142. Used by permission.
[5] Cambridge University Press, 1951, p. 235. Used by permission.

the knowledge of the infinite God there is no quantitative measure or limit. All consists in him and exists in his presence and is known by him. God, whom Christ revealed, is great enough to be the God of everything. All the planets are his too.

The Light of Everywhere

The Word which was incarnate in Christ is the light of everywhere. The prologue of the Gospel according to John contains a statement of what we may recognize as three movements or acts in the revelation of the Word. "The true light that enlightens every man was coming into the world." (John 1:9.) This must refer to a widely diffused activity of the Word throughout the whole pre-Christian history of the world. "He came to his own home, and his own people received him not." (John 1:11.) This seems clearly to mean the communication of the Word to the Jewish people through such media as the prophets. "And the Word became flesh and dwelt among us." (John 1:14.) This is the personal presence of the Word in the historical life of Jesus Christ. Thus the Word present in personal life in Christ was the same Word that had come to the people of Israel and that had been effective always throughout all the world.[6] In what way the movements or acts in the revelation of the Word may have taken place on other planets we can scarcely hope to know, but we cannot doubt that if on other planets there is life capable of responding to God and in need of God, then the Word has been effective and outreaching in those places as well as here. In the second volume of his *Systematic Theology*, in which he deals with "Existence and the Christ," Professor Paul Tillich remarks:

[6] For further discussion of the passage in John see William Robinson, *The Biblical Doctrine of the Church* (St. Louis: The Bethany Press, 1955), pp. 20-23.

"Man cannot claim to occupy the only possible place for Incarnation." Observing that if there are nonhuman worlds in which there is estrangement from God, "such worlds cannot be without the operation of saving power within them," he declares, "The expectation of the Messiah . . . presupposes that 'God loves the universe,' even though in the appearance of the Christ he actualizes this love for historical man alone."[7]

The Lord of Everything Everywhere

Can we go any farther than this? I believe we can. In the course of the argument just summarized, Professor Tillich himself states: "The interdependence of everything with everything else in the totality of being includes a participation of nature in history and demands a participation of the universe in salvation."[8] If then in the totality of being everything is interdependent with everything else, what Christ is and does, since it is the expression of God, is valid in relation to all that God has made. Even if God has spoken "in many and various ways" on other planets, there can be nothing inconsistent there with what he has said here to us in Christ. Indeed since Christ is God himself acting in human history, what God has done in Christ upon this small planet may be the very act by which God redeems the whole universe. The choice of this planet for this action is no more remarkable than the choice upon this planet of the Jewish people as the vehicle for the incarnation. Nothing less than this seems to be the claim of the New Testament, since Colossians 1:20 states that it is the purpose of God through Christ "to reconcile to himself all things, whether on earth or in heaven," and since in Revelation 1:16 the one

[7] Paul Tillich, *Systematic Theology*, II (Chicago: The University of Chicago Press, 1957), p. 96. Used by permission.
[8] *Ibid.*

like a son of man is pictured as holding in his right hand seven stars which, after ancient manner of thought, must mean the seven planets as then known.

Wherever we go in outer space, therefore, we may and we must carry the message and the good news about Jesus Christ. The first space ships will presumably be military vehicles, since only the military has the enormous resources with which to accomplish a mission into space. Some way must be found that these space ships will carry missionaries, and the only way which now appears is that there should be humble and simple Christians in the services from which the space voyagers are chosen. Perhaps young people who read these words will be among those assigned to such enviable missions. Wherever we go and in whatever place there is opportunity, we must tell that God has spoken thus to us upon earth in Jesus Christ.

CHAPTER 4

Cosmic Redemption

In this book so far we have seen how man in our time has begun to use the atom and to go up toward space. We have recognized these as the twin marks of the beginning of a new age, the nuclear-space age, an age both of amazing possibilities and of terrifying dangers. Because of the ambiguous character of this age, in the light of the Bible we must still call it a part, perhaps one of the last parts, of the old age, and we must still look toward the really new age, the age of the kingdom of God, which Christ came to bring to us. This we need most of all. In the nuclear-space age we naturally try to think of the work of Christ and the message of salvation in relation to the whole universe. When we do this, we are actually doing only what the Bible has done already, for it already speaks of redemption in cosmic terms.

A chief passage in which the cosmic scope of salvation is set forth is Romans 8:18-25. Here Paul speaks of the "creation," using a Greek word which means "that which has been created," and explicitly refers to "the whole creation," which must mean the sum total of everything made, the same as we mean when we refer to the "universe" or the "cosmos." As Paul looks upon the "whole creation," he sees in it certain tragic elements.

Tragic Elements in the Cosmos

The first of these is futility. "The creation," he says, "was subjected to futility." Futility is that which comes to nothing, does not get anywhere, is useless and vain. In some of its aspects the universe seems to be characterized by a failure to get anywhere. As was stated in classic way by Ecclesiastes, the same things just happen over and over: the sun rises and sets, the wind blows, the streams flow to the sea, "and there is nothing new under the sun."

Sometimes when you are playing a phonograph record the needle jumps out of the groove and goes back and plays the same thing over and over again. Perhaps it is a symphony which ought to go on toward a glorious conclusion, but instead the needle simply repeats the same phrase incessantly. That is how the universe sometimes impresses some people. Nature is a ceaseless repetition and history too, they think, only repeats the same cycles endlessly. In such observations there is enough of truth to make us recognize an apparent element of futility as a part of the tragic aspect of the cosmos.

Another tragic element in the universe is that of decay. In his same passage about the "whole creation" Paul speaks of its "bondage to decay." Everything grows old. Everything wears down and wears out. Ecclesiastes says that all the streams run to the sea, and we know that every stream which descends from the mountains to the ocean carries with it a bit of the hills. Thus we recognize that in general the more rounded mountains are the older ones, worn down in the course of time. Energy appears to be running down. The second law of thermodynamics states that when radiant energy or heat is interchanged between two bodies at different temperatures it is always the hotter which loses energy to the colder. As for man, he is "like grass," which flourishes in the morning but "in the evening . . . fades and withers." (Psalm 90:5-6.) There is apparent futility and there is evident decay in the universe. In "Ben Jonson Entertains a Man from Stratford," Edwin Arlington Robinson writes:

> It's all a world where bugs and emperors
> Go singularly back to the same dust,
> Each in his time; and the old, ordered stars
> That sang together, Ben, will sing the same
> Old stave tomorrow.[1]

The repetition of things and the decline of things of which the poet speaks are also recognized by the Bible. Although it also has much else to say, the Bible speaks realistically about the tragic aspects of the cosmos.

Yet another tragic element indicated by Paul is pain. "We know," he says, "that the whole creation has been groaning in travail together until now." Pain is one of the terrible facts of human life. Long-continued pain can be almost unbearable and lead to desperation. How far beyond man pain is felt in the universe it is difficult for us to know, but it exists at least in the realm of animal life. Even before Darwin's *Origin of Species* was published in 1859, Tennyson had written in 1850 of "Nature, red in tooth and claw." Asian religions may exaggerate the matter when they speak of pain in the realm of plant life, nevertheless the ranges of pain in the universe are broad, and Paul was sensitive to this fact when he seemed to hear the whole creation groaning as if in travail.

---

[1] *The Man Against the Sky* (New York: The Macmillan Company, 1916), p. 60. Used by permission.

Constructive Aspects of Tragic Elements

Christianity views the cosmos realistically, then, as pervaded by tragic elements and in need of redemption all together. Christianity not only leads us to be realistic in our thinking, however, but also helps us to have courage to see the constructive side of these otherwise tragic elements in the universe. It is indeed the greatest force in the world, as countless examples have shown, to help men tackle tragedy and turn it into triumph. Christianity lifts us above futilitarianism. The ceaseless repetitions of nature strike some as a meaningless vanity; they also in fact show forth a faithful regularity. While Ecclesiastes found monotony in the rising and setting of the sun, and derived a sense of weariness from the contemplation of it, the Psalmist looked at the same sun and saw it as resembling a strong man who runs his course with joy, and regarded it as one of the heavenly bodies which proclaim the glory of God. (Psalm 19:1-5.) Jesus in turn spoke of the sun and interpreted the regularity of its ascent in the sky as an expression of the impartial benevolence of God who "makes his sun rise on the evil and on the good." (Matthew 5:45.) As for the modern scientist, he looks at the same recurrence of natural happenings and finds precisely therein the opportunity for learning to work with the great forces which are round about us.

Decay is a part of everything that has been made, from the mountains to the flowers and including man in between. Yet the very process of disintegration releases power which apparently would not be available otherwise. On the scientific level, burning coal transmits its heat to water and illustrates the second law of thermodynamics that in the interchange of heat it is always the warmer object which loses energy to the cooler. But in the process the water is brought to the boiling point and made to give off steam which drives the machines of industry. Atomic fission is decay of the elements at an accelerated rate, but it releases prodigious power which becomes available for weal or woe. The decay of growing older seems to be the only way to gain wisdom—and even then some of us do not gain too much! But the price for the growth of the soul is the growing older of the body, and the Bible points to the splendid prospect that in advancing years

. . . the path of the righteous is like the light of dawn, which shines brighter and brighter until full day.—Proverbs 4:18.

As for pain, it will be observed in a later chapter that this is often the stimulus of progress. Both for men and also, as Arnold Toynbee has shown, for societies, comfort may lead to stagnation and decline, the threat of peril and pain may impel to vital action.

The Ultimate Hope

The final expectation of the Christian faith, however, is not just that some good can be wrested out of the tragic elements of existence, but rather that the tragic will itself be overcome in the ultimate consummation. The creation, Paul declares in the passage we have been studying, was subjected to futility "in hope," and the hope is that "the creation itself will be set free from its bondage to decay and obtain the glorious liberty of the children of God." Presumably therefore the very nature of the tragic elements in the universe must point to the nature of the triumph which is ahead when the redemptive purpose of God is worked out for the whole cosmos. If this is correct, then we may say that the sense of futility leads us to hope that someday the meaning of all things will be seen. It would indeed be wonderful sometime to know that nothing had transpired in vain, that everything had fitted into its place in a pattern which was greater than we knew at the time. Thus Tennyson felt keenly the pain of the world but he also expressed the splendid hope:

> O, yet, we trust that somehow good
>   Will be the final goal of ill,
>   To pangs of nature, sins of will,
> Defects of doubt, and taints of blood;

> That nothing walks with aimless feet;
>   That not one life shall be destroyed,
>   Or cast as rubbish to the void,
> When God hath made the pile complete.[2]

The poignant knowledge of decay points us likewise to the hope of permanence. Here the flower withers and all that is most precious must sometime slip out of our earthly hands. But the Bible speaks of faith and hope and love which abide. Since these are personal values persons must have an abiding place in the eternal purposes of God.

Yet again the experience of pain leads to the hope of joy. When travail is past the pain is quite forgotten in the gladness over what has come to be. This is the picture which Paul gives us. The whole vast universe is now groaning in pain because of the tragic elements within it, but some day it will all be made new and glorious and in that glory the former pain shall be quite forgotten. Nothing less than this is the splendid Christian hope of cosmic redemption.

[2] *In Memoriam*, LIV.

PART TWO:

The Nature of the Times

Chapter 5

Between the Times

In the preceding chapters we have said that the nuclear-space age is a remarkable new period in the history of man, yet so fraught with fear as well as buoyed with hope that it appears to us yet a part, even if a climactic part, of what the Bible would call the old age. At the same time we have affirmed that by biblical teaching the really new age, the age of the kingdom of God, has also already been inaugurated by Jesus Christ. What this latter affirmation means, for an understanding of the nature of our times, must now be investigated further.

What Has Happened

What has happened already is something wonderful. In the New Testament the message about what has happened is called the "Gospel," and the word "gospel" means "good news." The message which Jesus himself proclaimed is called by this term and was stated in the words, "The time is fulfilled, and the kingdom of God is at hand." (Mark 1: 14-15.) The word kingdom means both realm and reign, and in the Bible the emphasis is upon the actual sway and rule of God. That the time would come when God's rule

would be fully actualized even despite all the opposition of
men was the hope of the Old Testament. The time in which
evil still prevailed was the old age. The time in which God's
sway would be made fully manifest would be the new age.
It was, therefore, a tremendous affirmation for Jesus to declare that the kingdom of God was at hand. That which is
at hand may be at hand in time. This means that it is about
to take place, it is imminent. Presumably Jesus meant that
God's long-hoped-for kingdom was about to be realized.
That which is at hand can also be at hand in space. This
would mean that it is near, so near that one can almost reach
out and touch it. Perhaps Jesus also meant this, that the
kingdom was so close that men could lay hold on it or enter
into it if they wished. As a matter of fact, he sometimes
spoke of the kingdom as not only near but also already present. The establishment of the kingdom would necessarily
involve the overthrow of the power of evil, and in connection with the work of his disciples Jesus said in the language
of the time, "'I saw Satan fall like lightning from heaven.'"
(Luke 10:18.) In the belief of the time, the minions of Satan
were demons who afflicted men with disease and dementia.
Accordingly, the miracles of Jesus, in which in the power
of God he healed the demonized, were signs of the present
breaking in of the kingdom. "'If it is by the finger of God
that I cast out demons,'" he said, "'then the kingdom of
God has come upon you.'" (Luke 11:20; cf. Matthew 12:
28.) Presumably it was of this same great and long-antici-
pated entity, the kingdom of God, that Jesus was speaking
when in contrast with the failure of his contemporaries to
recognize what was in their midst he recalled how the queen
of Sheba came so far to hear the wisdom of Solomon, and
then said, "'Behold, something greater than Solomon is
here.'" (Matthew 12:42.)

A sign that this was really so was the work which Jesus

was doing. His miracles had such a significance, as already mentioned, and so did his message. When on one occasion he remarked that no sign would be given to the present generation "except the sign of the prophet Jonah," and then recalled how the men of Nineveh had repented at the preaching of Jonah,[1] his primary meaning must have been that his own preaching constituted the decisive sign for his contemporaries. If it was *his* deeds and *his* message which signaled the coming of the kingdom of God, then it was indeed his own presence, thus doing and thus speaking, which was the sign of the imminence and the anticipatory presence of that kingdom. It was as a matter of fact a widespread belief among the Jews that God would establish his kingdom through a person whom he would send. Since the Israelite king of olden times had been consecrated to his office by an act of anointing, it was anticipated that the divinely sent ruler of the new and hoped-for age would be the "anointed." In Hebrew this word is Messiah, and in Greek it is translated "Christ." It seems from the records in the first three Gospels, commonly called the Synoptic Gospels, that, at least in public speech, Jesus was very reticent about himself and any claims of his own. So much is this the case that some students of the records think that he himself never actually defined his own mission and person as that of the Messiah. Perhaps this was because the title Messiah would have suggested a worldly kingship and even a program of revolutionary violence to many of his contemporaries. Nevertheless the records indicate that people about him, particularly including his immediate followers, came to believe that he was in fact the expected Christ. In the synagogue at Capernaum "a man with an unclean spirit" cried out to him, "I know who you are, the Holy One of God." (Mark 1:23-24.) Later the disciples said to him

[1] Cf. Matthew 12:39, 41; Luke 11:29, 32; Matthew 16:4.

through their spokesman, Peter, "You are the Christ." And, according to Mark 14:61-62, near the end of his life he himself answered the interrogation of the high priest, "Are you the Christ?" with the plain reply, "I am." Whether or not he used the title of the Christ, Jesus certainly seems to have spoken with complete and unhesitating authority about the kingdom of God. As a recent writer puts it: "His authority spoke for itself. And it is on this inherent authority, rather than on any titles that he or others may have used to describe his vocation, that the Christian can most surely base his faith in Jesus as the incarnate Son of God."[2]

Yet precisely this unmistakable authority must always lead to the question as to who Jesus is. Commenting on the Sermon on the Mount, R. W. Dale once phrased the interrogations which arise from a serious consideration of these tremendous teachings as follows:

Who is this that places persecution for his sake side by side with persecution for righteousness' sake, and declares that whether men suffer for loyalty to him or for loyalty to righteousness they are to receive their reward in the divine kingdom? Who is it that in that sermon places his own authority side by side with the authority of God, and gives to the Jewish people and to all mankind new laws which require a deeper and more inward righteousness than was required by the Ten Commandments? Who is it that in that sermon assumes the awful authority of pronouncing final judgment on men? . . . These are not words that we ever heard before or have ever heard since, from teacher or prophet. Who is he? That question cannot be silenced when words like these have once been spoken.

Jesus, we conclude, thought of his own work as messianic in nature, and his followers believed that Jesus was the Christ and in fact were known as "Christians." Thus the confession that Jesus is the Christ remains a proper expression of the faith of those who believe that in Jesus the kingdom of God drew near and was in fact already present. Paul Tillich sums

[2] Sherman E. Johnson, *Jesus in His Homeland* (New York: Charles Scribner's Sons, 1957), p. 143. Quoted by permission.

up the Christian message for our time with the words: "Christianity is the message of the New Creation, the New Being, the New Reality which has appeared with the appearance of Jesus who for this reason, and just for this reason, is called the Christ. For the Christ, the Messiah, the selected and anointed one is He who brings the new state of things."[3]

The kingdom of God has drawn near and the Christ has come—these are two of the marks of what has already happened. But yet a third thing has also already taken place, and this is something which has transpired in the lives of those who have heard this message and accepted it. There are different ways in which this third happening is spoken of in the New Testament, and some of them are as follows. Those who have heeded the message about the kingdom have been sanctified. When John the Baptist declared that judgment was at hand and that after him was coming the one who was mightier than he, he proceeded to dip into the Jordan River those who accepted this proclamation. When Peter told about Jesus Christ and men asked what they should do, the apostle instructed them to "repent, and be baptized." This immersion in water of those who accepted the message of the imminence of the kingdom and the significance of Jesus as the Christ was a natural symbol of inward cleansing. Already in the Dead Sea Scrolls of the Qumran community, which may have had some connection with the movements of John the Baptist and of Jesus, it was said of a person of stubbornness of heart that he cannot purify himself by any ablution,

> Nor sanctify himself with seas or rivers,
> Nor cleanse himself with any water for washing![4]

[3] Paul Tillich, *The New Being* (New York: Charles Scribner's Sons, 1955), p. 15. Used by permission.

[4] *The Manual of Discipline* (1QS), III, 5.

The reason this cleansing was necessary was that God, whose kingdom was about to come, was, according to the teaching already long maintained in the Old Testament, a God of holiness. Therefore those who would be in his kingdom must be made clean. So the Christians, like the followers of John the Baptist before them, were washed in the outward waters of baptism to signify their willingness and desire to be cleansed in the inward places of the heart. Since this was universal early Christian practice, and since in the relationship to Christ which was thereby inaugurated people actually experienced an inward renovation, Paul could call the Christians at Corinth collectively "those sanctified in Christ Jesus," and could say to them as of something which had already taken place, "you were washed, you were sanctified." (1 Corinthians 1:2; 6:11.)

Another New Testament way of stating what has already happened to the Christian is to say that he has been justified. Here the language moves from the symbol of ablution to the realm of the law court. If the coming of God's kingdom will also mean the coming of God's judgment, a judgment which John the Baptist described as a laying of the ax to the root of the trees so that every tree which does not bear good fruit shall be cut down and thrown into the fire, man must indeed regard with the utmost seriousness the prospect which is before him. Only righteousness can stand in the presence of the righteous God, and what man can appear before God and maintain his own sufficient righteousness? The conscience, the Gentiles widely believed, was a guide to what was right, and the Law, the Jews held, provided an explicit statement of the divine requirements, but to a sensitive person like Paul who knew both the Greek and the Jewish worlds, there was "none . . . righteous" to be found in either world. Indeed, it was his own experience that the Law itself, although it was "holy and just and good," worked in fact to heighten the awareness of sin, to stimulate with its prohibitions the tendency to transgress, and to confront man with the impossible task of achieving salvation by his own works. How, then, can man have righteousness if, as universal experience shows, he cannot obtain it by his own effort? Paul's answer is that God, out of his own goodness and on the basis of what Jesus has done, declares righteous those who have loving trust in him through Christ. Man's situation is here pictured, as we have said, in terms of the law court and the solution of the problem is stated in a term which is to be understood within the framework of that forum, that is in a forensic sense. The righteousness which man does not possess as an ethical quality of his own accomplishing, he does receive as a verdict from God who pronounces him acceptable even though he is unacceptable. Thus the word "justify," which is the usual translation of the Greek term Paul uses in this connection, while it means most simply "to make right," is characteristically employed by Paul with the sense, "to pronounce and treat as righteous." This is what God, in his goodness and on account of the work of Christ, does, and faith is the trustful acceptance of this verdict, a verdict which could never be earned by one's own attainment. As Paul states it in Romans 4:5, "And to one who does not work but trusts him who justifies the ungodly, his faith is reckoned as righteousness." Like sanctification discussed in the preceding paragraph and to which it is much akin,[5] justification belongs to the initiation of the Christian life, and Paul regularly says that Christians have been justified. "Therefore, since we are justified by faith . . ." he writes in the first verse of the fifth chapter of Romans, and in verse nine

[5] See J. K. S. Reid in Alan Richardson, ed., *A Theological Word Book of the Bible* (New York: The Macmillan Company, 1951), p. 218.

says again, "Since, therefore, we are now justified by his blood. . . ."

The person who, on the ground of faith in God through Christ, has been sanctified and justified may also, in New Testament language, be said to have been saved. Paul speaks thus in Romans 8:24 where he says, "For in this hope we were saved." Also in other letters bearing his name but believed by some to have been written by later followers of his rather than by Paul himself, we find these statements: "By grace you have been saved" (Ephesians 2:5); "He saved us, not because of deeds done by us in righteousness, but in virtue of his own mercy, by the washing of regeneration and renewal in the Holy Spirit." (Titus 3:5.)

Here then we have uncovered the real dividing point of the ages as it is represented in the New Testament. In the time of Jesus the kingdom of God drew near and in his words and works its power was felt as an already present reality. Those who put their trust in God on the basis of what Jesus Christ said and did have the assurance that they have received already the sanctification and justification and salvation which for so long were hoped for for the future. This is what has already happened.

The Completion of What Has Been Begun

Yet at every point that which has already taken place represents only a beginning and is not yet a completion. The kingdom of God has drawn near and begun to break in, but it has not yet come fully. Otherwise Jesus would not have taught his disciples to pray to the Father in heaven, "Thy kingdom come." That is a supplication for something which is not yet. At least in the version of the prayer found in Matthew, these words are followed in characteristic Semitic parallelism by another statement of the same re-

quest, "Thy will be done," and both of these formulations
of the entreaty are then qualified by the words, "On earth
as it is in heaven." This shows that the object of request is
the realization of the full reign of God, and that this is
expected upon this earth. That greatly to-be-desired consummation certainly lies yet in the future. As we see all
the woes of the world—refugees trudging along their lonely
way, criminals involved in a tangled net of circumstances,
and people suffering pain and sorrow—we feel that it assuredly cannot be the will of God that these things are so.
His will is not yet done on earth as it is in heaven.

Likewise the New Testament which tells us of the coming
of Jesus as the Christ also looks forward to his coming
again. The word which is used in this connection means
literally "a being present." The thought here attested is
that Christ is not now fully and manifestly present in the
world. In what manner his full and manifest "being present"
is to be conceived it is not easy to say, yet that the Christian
hope cannot fail to include this expectation seems evident.
In Hellenistic Greek the word of which we are speaking
is often used of the arrival of a king, an event for which
every possible preparation must be made in advance.[6]
Christians must prepare for the being present of their King,
and Paul prays for the Thessalonians: "And may the Lord
make you increase and abound in love to one another and
to all men, as we do to you, so that he may establish your
hearts unblamable in holiness before our God and Father,
at the coming of our Lord Jesus with all his saints." (1
Thessalonians 3:12-13.)

Furthermore, while it can be said that Christians have
been sanctified, justified, and saved, it is evident, and sometimes it is all too painfully evident, that what has been

[6] See William Barclay, A New Testament Wordbook (New York:
Harper & Brothers, no date), p. 91.

begun in them for good has not yet been brought to its completion. Sanctification is first of all a status which is conferred upon us in Christ, but it is also something which we are earnestly to bestir ourselves to obtain. Paul could say to the Corinthians, "You were washed, you were sanctified," but he could also urge them, "Let us cleanse ourselves from every defilement of body and spirit, and make holiness perfect in the fear of God." We may say, therefore, that the Christian has been sanctified but in his sanctification is not yet perfected. Yet his assurance is that if he allows and earnestly seeks the furtherance of what has been begun, this will be carried to a good end. Paul expresses this assurance in another passage in these words: "And I am sure that he who began a good work in you will perfect it until the day of Jesus Christ."

Likewise we may say that the Christian has been justified but is not yet fully glorified. The glory of God was in the face of Christ, as Paul declares in 2 Corinthians 4:6, and after his earthly life he was "taken up in glory," as what may be an early Christian hymn quoted in 1 Timothy 3:16 states. The followers of Christ, to whom is given the great privilege of beholding his glory, even now "are being changed into his likeness from one degree of glory to another," and may properly feel assured that it is their destiny at last to be conformed to his image, a conformation and a transformation in which the Savior "will change our lowly body to be like his glorious body." Since in his present "lowly body" the believer still belongs to the world as it is, and since this world is everywhere marked by travail, he must often experience suffering. But this was the experience of Christ too, and it must be expected by his followers. Indeed it is only if we share his sufferings that we may expect to share his glory. The statement of this truth by Paul in Romans 8:17—"provided we suffer with him in order that we may

also be glorified with him"—shows plainly that while the
suffering is a present experience, the full glorification is an
object of hope and expectation for the future. It is true that
in Romans 8:30 Paul speaks of those whom God predestined,
called, justified, and glorified, but in this case he is thinking
of these successive steps as they would appear in the fore-
knowledge of God and it is for this reason that he uses the
past tense in all the verbs. From our own time-limited point
of view the Christian has already been called and justified
but not yet fully glorified.

Yet again, the word "saved" must be related to the
future as well as to the past. Even where Paul uses the past
tense as plainly as he does in Romans 8:24, he also refers
to hope which points to the future: "In this hope we were
saved." Elsewhere, in a way which seems to be most characteristic of his thought as a whole, he clearly indicates
that salvation is something to be expected and awaited in
a time yet to come. Thus in Romans 5:9, for example, justification is clearly something which has been received, but
salvation is something which is yet awaited and expected:
"Since, therefore, we are now justified by his blood, much
more shall we be saved by him from the wrath of God."

The Character of the Present Time

Accordingly, the situation of the Christian must be described as that of living between the times. The Christian
has been delivered from the old, but is not yet in full possession of the new. He may know that he has been saved,
but he must also hope that he will be saved, and perhaps
the simplest way to state his position is to use the phrase
found in Acts 2:47 and say that he is "being saved."

The war, to state the matter in another way, has been
won, yet the war is still going on. Oscar Cullmann has illustrated the matter by pointing out that in warfare the

Entscheidungsschlacht, that is the decisive battle, may occur in a comparatively early phase of the struggle and may not even be recognized by all as such at the time. The warfare may still continue a long while until the final victory day when, in fact, the turning point came long before. So in what Christ has done the decisive battle has been won, yet the Christian is still engaged in the conflict.[7] D. T. Niles says essentially the same thing when he writes of the message brought by Christianity: "The call of the evangelist is not so much that men should engage in a battle with evil until evil is destroyed, as that they should share in God's victory over evil until evil is exposed. The Gospel is a call to a battle whose final victory is already won."[8]

Or, as yet another statement of the situation may be phrased, the Christian has peace, yet is not out of peril. "We have peace"—this Paul can state unequivocally;[9] yet he can also urge with all earnestness: "work out your own salvation with fear and trembling." (Philippians 2:12.) "We tremble at the thought of eternity, and well we may," wrote Jean Nicolas Grou, "but if the fear was turned to good account, we should soon learn to rejoice in trembling." Rejoicing in trembling! This well describes the Christian who lives between the times.

The responsibility of the Christian also becomes evident in the light of the foregoing. We should receive what is given us but also strive for what is yet to come to us.

To put it in another way, we live in the indicative, yet

[7] See *Christus und die Zeit* (Zürich: Evangelischer Verlag A. G. Zollikon, 1946), pp. 72f.

[8] *That They May Have Life* (New York: Harper & Brothers, 1951), pp. 20-21. Used by permission.

[9] Romans 5:1. The indicative "we have peace" (Revised Standard Version text) as opposed to the subjunctive "let us have peace" (Revised Standard Version margin) is now supported by the oldest parchment fragment of Romans, the third-century Wyman manuscript known as 0220.

also under the imperative. The indicative is the description
of what is, the imperative is the command leading to what
ought to be. Thus Paul says of our baptism that in it we
were buried with Christ into death, making a positive statement about what has happened; but in the conclusion of
the sentence he writes of what is now privilege and possibility, namely, "that as Christ was raised from the dead
. . . we too might walk in newness of life." (Romans 6:4.)
So, too, in virtually every letter Paul writes first a statement
of what is, according to Christian doctrine, and then in the
latter part of the letter moves into exhortations relative to
what ought to be and what must be.

CHAPTER 6

Myopia in Utopia

In the foregoing we have seen that in the words and work of Jesus as the Christ what the New Testament calls the kingdom of God and what a philosophical theologian calls the New Reality has drawn near and has indeed appeared in human history. It is, therefore, important to see what is already here, and it was in fact a concern of Jesus that men did not so see. "Are your hearts hardened?" he asked. "Having eyes do you not see, and having ears do you not hear?" (Mark 8:18.)

They Did Not See

Since, as we have seen, Jesus said that the kingdom of God was at hand, and did deeds which showed that it had really arrived, and since he was himself the sign thereof, how was it that men did not realize what was in their midst? For one thing, as the remark of Jesus about this situation points out, they simply did not see what was there to be seen. "Having eyes do you not see?" Such failure to see may be due to shortsightedness. Myopia, as this is technically called, is a condition of the eye in which the rays of light from a distant object are brought to a focus before they reach the retina, and thus form an indistinct image. So if your friend does not give you the salutation you expect from across the street, it may be because you are a blur rather than a sharp image on the retina of his myopic eye. In relation to the kingdom of God many of the people of Jesus' day were afflicted with myopic vision. They were looking at things which were not very far away, but they still could not see far enough to see the kingdom of God. The innkeeper at Bethlehem was too shortsightedly occupied and preoccupied with his overcrowded hostelry to have any clear vision of who Mary and Joseph were when they knocked in need upon his door, and because of that "there was no place for them in the inn." The people of whom Jesus told in his parable of the great banquet of the kingdom missed out on the opportunity to participate in that great occasion, although freely invited, just because of preoccupation with very immediate matters. " ' "I have bought a field, and I must go out and see it," said one; "I have bought five yoke of oxen, and I go to examine them," said another; "I have married a wife, and therefore I cannot come," ' " said a third. (Luke 14:18-20.) Thus they lost the place they might have had, and others came in their stead. Likewise Martha, "distracted with much serving," failed to seize the opportunity which Mary took of listening to the teaching of Jesus.

Another condition of the eyes which also makes correct seeing difficult is farsightedness. The farsighted person can see things in the distance but not near at hand. The time comes when he cannot hold a book far enough from himself to read the print in it. This also was true of some of the contemporaries of Jesus in regard to the kingdom of God. They were looking for it in the far distance and could not recognize it when it was close to them. They were expecting a conqueror on a war horse, and could not recognize the significance of the child at Bethlehem. They were looking for one to hold the Great Assize, and they overlooked the importance of the one who declined to be "a judge or divider" among them. They scanned the clouds for the Son

of man who was expected there, but they did not understand the Son of man who trudged their dusty roads and had
"nowhere to lay his head."

The presence of the kingdom was also missed because
people did not hear what was to be heard. "Having ears do
you not hear?" asked Jesus. As he taught, Jesus would frequently conclude a saying or a story with the words: "He
who has ears to hear, let him hear." He used these words
at the conclusion of his parable of the sower, then afterward remarked that the reason he spoke in parables was
"so that they may indeed see but not perceive, and may indeed hear but not understand." This is followed in Matthew's report of the event by the quotation of the prophecy
of Isaiah (6:9-10) which says:

> "'You shall indeed hear but never understand,
>   and you shall indeed see but never perceive.
> For this people's heart has grown dull,
>   and their ears are heavy of hearing,
>   and their eyes they have closed,
> lest they should perceive with their eyes,
>   and hear with their ears,
> and understand with their heart,
>   and turn for me to heal them.'"
>
>   —Matthew 13:14-15

It may seem rather surprising that Jesus would say that he
told parables in order that people would hear them and not
understand, and some students feel that this is a reflection
of early Christian thought about the apparent failure of
the teaching of Jesus rather than a report of what he himself ever said. The citation of the Old Testament prophecy
reminds us, however, of the manner of thought in ancient
Israel where, as H. D. A. Major has pointed out,[1] men did

[1] H. D. A. Major, T. W. Manson, and C. J. Wright, *The Mission
and Message of Jesus* (New York: E. P. Dutton and Co., Inc., 1938),
p. 70.

not distinguish between the effect of God's action and its intention. If a certain result followed, that result must have been what was intended in the first place. It was only in that sense, we may hold, that Jesus told parables "so that" people might not understand. The effect is stated as if it were the intention. Surely his parables were told in order to communicate truth and give free men an opportunity to lay hold on it, only the result was that they failed to comprehend it and to apprehend it.

Yet another way of stating how it was that men missed the kingdom in their midst is to say that they did not feel it. "Are your hearts hardened?" Jesus asked wistfully. From the time that Mary was turned away from the door of the inn at Bethlehem to the time when Jesus hung upon the cross and "those who passed by derided him," so that he might well have asked, "Is it nothing to you, all you who pass by?" hardness of heart played its damaging part in the missing and the rejecting of the kingdom.

We Do Not See

For the same reasons we continue to miss the important things of the kingdom of God. We do not see. We may be too shortsighted.

A robber has told the story of his brilliant and dashing career in crime. He was a man of great ability and he was able to lay his hands illicitly upon many treasures. He seized the opportunites which presented themselves immediately before him. But when he looked back over his life he finally had to say, "The only one I robbed was myself." While it is scarcely true that he had not caused loss to others, it is certainly true that he had caused the greatest of loss to himself by the shortness of his vision.

It is also possible to miss the things that are really important by looking too far into the distance. Count Tolstoy undoubtedly envisioned some of the glorious things of the kingdom of God, yet his wife wrote of how he failed ever to give her any help in her arduous tasks at home.

Sometimes we do not hear. The range of our hearing is limited and the magnitude of some sounds is too great for us. There is the thunder of revolution in the world as peoples long subject are becoming nations, and races long denied justice are claiming their rights, but some, even statesmen, cannot hear the portentous sounds. On the other hand there are some sounds too slight for our notice, like the whisper of a purpose, the murmur of conscience, or the still, small voice of God.

And sometimes we do not feel. As the hand develops callouses from repeated contact with rough surfaces, so the heart builds up a protective covering against what would touch it. Yet the dinosaurs which were best insulated from the world by almost impervious protective coverings, perished, and man whose nerves were sensitively near the surface of his tender skin and thus most exposed to the feeling of pain, learned thereby to share the experiences of his fellows and developed a society which lived. As John Ruskin wrote: "He only is advancing in life whose heart is getting softer, whose blood warmer, whose brain quicker, whose spirit is entering into living peace."

How to See the Kingdom

The same words of Jesus which remind us that the kingdom of God is often not perceived although already present, also point to ways in which to heighten awareness of it. It is important to appreciate our possession of capabilities by which to respond to God's world and God's word. There is light and color in the world, and we are normally provided with eyes responsive to the wave lengths of that light. There is sound and melody, and we have ears which may hear it. Indeed, those whose sight or hearing is impaired may so heighten the use of other senses as to be more keenly aware than many others of some of the beauties of the world. There are people all about us, and we naturally have feelings which, if not suppressed and crushed, bring us into empathy with them. God is, and there exists within man the capacity to respond to him.

It is important not only to remember our possession of these capacities but also to realize our responsibility for the use of them. While in the ancient Israelite way of thought, the prophets and perhaps Jesus, too, spoke of the result that men did not hear God's word as if that were the divine intention, it is unmistakable in many of the biblical passages that men are being summoned to give heed to what may be heard and understood if they earnestly wish. Thus Jeremiah appealed:

> "Hear this, O foolish and senseless people,
>   who have eyes, but see not,
>   who have ears, but hear not."
>
> —Jeremiah 5:21

Similarly Ezekiel called the people "a rebellious house, who have eyes to see, but see not, who have ears to hear, but hear not." (Ezekiel 12:2.) And in a passage already quoted it was said:

> " 'For this people's heart has grown dull,
>   and their ears are heavy of hearing,
>   and their eyes they have closed.' "
>
> —Matthew 13:15

In all of these statements it certainly seems indicated that we have something to do with whether our eyes see and our ears hear and our hearts are sensitive. Thus the poet takes as the title of his poem the words of Isaiah, "Lest They See with Their Eyes," and writes:

> You do not even care to know
> If Jesus' word is yes or no.

You close your eyes lest you may see
A young man hanging on a tree.

You close your ears lest you may hear
Insistently a clarion clear.

Though God Himself should die for you,
You do just what you choose to do.[2]

We need, then, to see and hear and understand. We need
to look at the world as wonderful. "The great difference,
intellectually speaking," Gilbert Murray has somewhere
written, "between one man and another is simply the
number of things they can see in a given cubic yard of
world." In this as in other things little children may often
be our guides to the kingdom of heaven. In *You Are Never
Alone*, Lowell Russell Ditzen has described the wonder of
a child at the things seen on a shopping trip with her
father to the neighboring village:

Hand in hand we started from the back door toward the car in the
barn. On that brief trek she had to stop to pat the dog good-by, break
away to try to catch a butterfly, pause under the cottonwood tree to
watch the way the wind was shaking the leaves, and study a cater-
pillar who piously humped his way across our path. . . .
"When and why," I asked myself, "do we let living stop being
fun? . . . Why do we quit observing and asking questions? How can
we permit the precious, powerful self that wonders and ponders and
appreciates, to be suffocated?"[3]

Thus the poet has written:

If such a tragic thing should come to pass
That I no more could thrill to wind-blown grass

[2] Charles Granville Hamilton in *The Christian-Evangelist*, Oct. 1,
1936, p. 1274. Used by permission.
[3] New York: Henry Holt and Company, 1956, pp. 107, 108-109.
Used by permission.

Or singing birds, or glory of the stars . . .
If I should see only the grief and scars
Of life, my poor soul blind to all earth's beauty
The while it bore its load of care and duty —
Or if my heart should flaunt unseemly pride
In its own weak success — then walk beside
Me, Lord, and show to me at eventide
The wonder of the universe and skies,
O, great Creator, open thou mine eyes![4]

We need to look at Jesus as the Christ. Long ago Simeon, an aged man who had been "looking for the consolation of Israel," saw the child Jesus brought into the temple and cried:

"Lord, now lettest thou thy servant depart in peace,
     according to thy word;
for mine eyes have seen thy salvation."
                              —Luke 2:29-30

We need to look at other people, even the least, as his brethren. "Our only hope of salvation, socially," Halford E. Luccock somewhere has written, "is in the increase in the number of open ears, alert to catch the cries of anguish and suffering."

So, looking in these and other ways we may catch glimpses of the presence of the kingdom of God, and of opportunities for service in it, all around us even now.

---

[4] Helen Miller Lehman, "Open Thou Mine Eyes," in *The Christian Century*, Oct. 8, 1947, p. 1201. Copyright 1947 Christian Century Foundation. Reprinted by permission.

CHAPTER 7

Foretaste of the Future

At this point in our investigation we are still studying the New Testament affirmation that the new age, to which men have long looked forward, really began with Jesus Christ. This does not mean that the hoped-for future of the completely realized sway of God in the world is as yet wholly here, but it does mean that in Jesus Christ that future has already had an effective beginning. Jesus himself indicated that it was only because men refused to see with their eyes and hear with their ears that they were unable to recognize the signs of the kingdom, signs which were present in his own words and works. Afterward the early Christians looked back upon the life of Christ as the dividing point of the times, and felt in their own experience the powers of the new age at work. Just how this is spoken of by some of the New Testament writers we must now notice.

Misconceptions

First, however, we may remark that there seem to be some misconceptions concerning the Christian outlook toward the future. In fact the Christian himself is confronted by nothing less than twin perils in regard to the future and the new age. These are that he may be too much preoccupied with the future, or that he may be quite unmindful of it. It is often supposed that Christians are characteristically engrossed and absorbed in thought of the future. This is frequently the charge of opponents of Christianity. The Christian faith is supposed to be something which dulls the sensitiveness of men to the troubles of the present by focusing their thoughts on the glories of a supposedly imaginary future. Similarly the rivals of Christianity sometimes suggest that the orientation of Christianity is so exclusively toward the future that the faith is not relevant to the present. In China many years ago I heard it said: "The teachings of Christ are for the next world. The teachings of Confucius are for this world." If such a view represents a caricature by the opponents of Christianity and an argument by its rivals, it is also sometimes a misapprehension on the part of its adherents. Some, to judge by their actions at least, regard Christianity as a doctrine which renders life unpleasant now, but which is to be endured in its unpleasant demands because of its promise of future bliss.

More widespread no doubt, at least in the earlier part of the twentieth century, was the inclination to concentrate so completely upon the tasks of the present that any thought of a goal lying at the end of history or beyond history was quite omitted.

But what is actually taught in the New Testament is something more remarkable, namely, that the Christian already has in some measure an experience of the future. Therefore he need not be excessively preoccupied with the future, neither can he doubt it.

Conceptions in the New Testament

One way in which the idea we are discussing is set forth in the New Testament is in the conception of the "earnest." This appears in the following passages in the King James Version. Second Corinthians 1:22 speaks of God "who hath also sealed us, and given the earnest of the Spirit in our hearts." Second Corinthians 5:5 refers to God "who also hath given unto us the earnest of the Spirit." Ephesians 1:13 mentions Christ "in whom also after that ye believed, ye were sealed with that holy Spirit of promise, which is the earnest of our inheritance until the redemption of the purchased possession." The word which is translated here as "earnest" appears already in the Old Testament. In Hebrew it is *êrabon,* and it is found, for example, in Genesis 38:17 where both the King James Version and the Revised Standard Version translate it as "pledge." In this case Judah has promised to give Tamar a kid from his flock, and she asks, "Will you give me a pledge, till you send it?" When he inquires what pledge she wants, Tamar replies, "Your signet and your cord, and your staff that is in your hand." These were probably a ring with a setting carved to make a distinctive impression when used as a seal, and carried ordinarily on a string about the neck, and a handstick no doubt beautifully carved and ornamented. These were given to Tamar for the time being as an *êrabon* or "pledge," doubtless legally binding, that the promised kid would in due time be forthcoming. In Greek we find the same word in the form *arrabōn,* and this is the word which occurs in the passages in 2 Corinthians and Ephesians cited above. It is found frequently in ancient authors, inscriptions, and papyri, where it means the deposit, down payment, or first installment in a legal or commercial transaction. By paying part of the purchase price in advance, the purchaser secures his claim to the object in question, and at the same time obligates himself to make the further specified payments. From Greek the word entered the vocabulary of Roman law in the form *arrhabo*, and eventually in English it was translated as "earnest." The idea is found throughout the history of law, wherever an agreement is made binding by the action of the buyer in giving something of value to the seller. In early Germanic practice the buyer gave something to the seller in return for his promise not to sell to anyone else. If the buyer wished to withdraw from the agreement he had to forfeit what he had put up for the option; if the seller defaulted he had to repay the advance payment double. In English law the payment bound both buyer and seller in a valid contract of sale, and under Edward I this initial deposit was known as "God's penny" and involved a religious obligation.

This, now, enables us to appreciate the remarkable idea set forth in the New Testament passages quoted above. At the outset of the Christian life God has given the believer the valuable gift of the Holy Spirit. The fact that he has done this already is the guarantee that he will also in the future give all the other benefits which are a part of complete salvation. In elucidating the idea of the *arrabōn* or "earnest" we have just used the word "guarantee," and this is indeed preferred as the translation of the term in the Revised Standard Version in the three New Testament passages quoted above. Of these the last and fullest, Ephesians 1:13-14, is translated thus in the Revised Standard Version: "You . . . were sealed with the promised Holy Sprit, which is the guarantee of our inheritance until we acquire possession of it."

Another way in which essentially the same idea is expressed in the New Testament is in the conception of the foretaste. This will not need such lengthy explanation for most of us are familiar with the idea of tasting something in advance. Many people find it pleasant to stand in the kitchen and get small samples of the cooking ahead of time. It is even reported that some cooks have gained much weight by having to taste what they were preparing to be sure that it was made right. We know what it means to get a taste ahead of time of what we are to enjoy more fully later. It is not surprising, then, that the conception of the foretaste occurs in the New Testament. In the picture-language often used to express expectations about the end-time, both Jewish and Christian sources often refer to the messianic meal or the heavenly banquet. Thus in the Dead Sea Scrolls the work known as "A Manual of Discipline for the Future Congregation of Israel" gives a description of the common meal of the community in the future, at which the priest will pronounce the blessing over bread and wine and stretch out his hand to the food, after which the anointed one will put forth his hand to it, and in turn all the members of the community will do likewise.[1] Jesus himself at the Last Supper with his apostles is recorded to have referred to the future meal in which he would again eat and drink with his disciples: "I have earnestly desired to eat this passover with you before I suffer; for I tell you I shall not eat it (or never eat it again) until it is fulfilled in the kingdom of God. . . . I tell you that from now on I shall not drink of the fruit of the vine until the kingdom of God comes." Likewise in the early Christian paintings in the catacombs at Rome we often see a group about a table on which are bread, wine, and fish, and this may portray the heavenly meal. Since the blessedness of the ultimate kingdom of God could be

[1] Theodor H. Gaster, *The Dead Sea Scriptures* (Garden City: Doubleday Anchor Books, 1956), p. 310.

pictured like this, it was natural to speak of the presently enjoyed benefits of the Christian life as a foretaste of what was yet to come fully. It is language of this sort which we find in Hebrews 6:4-5 where the Christians are described as "those who have once been enlightened, who have tasted the heavenly gift, and have become partakers of the Holy Spirit, and have tasted the goodness of the word of God and the powers of the age to come."

Yet again we find the conception of the first fruits. In the agricultural economy of ancient Palestine the harvest was very important. An archeological object, a limestone tablet believed to be nearly as old as 1000 B.C. and known as the Gezer Calendar, gives a list of the twelve months of the year and the agricultural work done in the several months. Two months of the fall are devoted to olive harvest, two months of the spring to harvest of grain. These were important times of the year. From an early period Israelite law required that when harvest began the first part of it was to be offered to the Lord. In Palestine the barley harvest begins in the spring at about the same time as the passover feast. Accordingly in the law found in the twenty-third chapter of Leviticus we are told about the passover which is held on the fourteenth day of the first month, Nisan, and then it is prescribed that on the day after the sabbath the priest shall wave before the Lord the sheaf of first fruits which the people have brought from the harvest. Fifty days later, at Pentecost, when the harvest is complete, they shall present a cereal offering of new grain to the Lord. Later the first fruit offerings were taken from all the "seven kinds," as they were called, or principal products of the land as named in Deuteronomy 8:8, wheat, barley, vines, fig trees, pomegranates, olive trees, and honey. Philo tells of the merriment and festivity when the people came to Jerusalem bringing these gifts. So complex, indeed, did the legal provisions concerning first fruits become that in the Jewish Mishna the entire tractate *Bikkurim* is devoted to this subject. The essence of the matter, however, is plain. The initial ingathering carried with it the promise of more to come; the first of the harvest at its very beginning was the promise of the fullness of the harvest at the time of its completion. Therefore when this symbolism is employed to describe that which the Christian enjoys even now, it points also to the greater fullness of blessing confidently to be expected in the endtime. Thus it is that Paul speaks of Christians in Romans 8:23 and says, "We . . . have . . . the first fruits of the Spirit."

The Earnest of the Spirit

Where, then, is the earnest or the foretaste or the first fruit of the future to be found? In all of the verses we have cited which express the ideas here under consideration there is mention of the Spirit. The statement of 2 Corinthians 1:22 that God "has . . . given us his Spirit in our hearts as a guarantee" shows that the earnest of the future is known by Christians in individual life. The presence of the Spirit in the hearts of believers brings such fruit as love, joy, peace, patience, kindness, goodness, faithfulness, gentleness, and self-control. (Galatians 5:22-23) These qualities of character are such as belong to the kingdom of God and the age to come, and here they are already present, at least in some measure, in the lives of Christian believers.

Again in the passage in Hebrews 6:4-5 the tasting of the heavenly gift and the partaking of the Holy Spirit are linked. Here the address seems to be to the whole church, possibly the church at Rome according to one interpretation of the destination of the epistle, and we have seen how in the Roman catacomb paintings a meal scene is often represented. Since the catacombs were primarily burial places of the early Christians this scene is presumably expressive of the Christian hope and may be interpreted as a depiction of the anticipated heavenly meal. Yet the elements which are shown on the table—fish, bread, and wine—are such as were partaken of by Jesus and his disciples in their common meals, and so there may well be allusion here, too, to those meals and to the observance of the communion service in the church. As Christians partake together of the Lord's Supper, they experience a fellowship which is a foretaste of the blessedness of the heavenly community.

In 1782 John and Mary Fawcett went to the leadership of the Baptist Church in Wainsgate, England. The meeting house held one hundred people, more when they built a gallery later. The congregation was composed of farmers and shepherds, all poor. The salary of the minister was 20 pounds a year, roughly one hundred dollars. Later when John and Mary had four children this was raised to 25 pounds, provided they could take out the raise in wool and potatoes. At their table they had porridge for breakfast, potatoes for dinner and supper. John was a faithful pastor, and he and his wife were loved by the congregation. He baptized the children, married the youth, buried the dead, and entered into deep associations with his people. Then came a call to a church in London which offered what appeared a wider opportunity and provided a larger salary. John preached his farewell sermon. The family's belongings were loaded onto a two-wheeled cart. The people of the church came to say good-by. Neither John nor Mary could leave. They unpacked the cart. They stayed for what was a fifty-four year ministry all together in Wainsgate and nearby Belden Bridge. On the Saturday night of the week in which he had almost left, John Fawcett wrote down some words and on Sunday morning the congregation sang them together. Although afterward King George III offered John

Fawcett any benefit in recognition of his work, and although Brown University conferred upon him the Doctor of Divinity degree, one cannot doubt that the most precious thing in all his life was that which he expressed in the words written on the Saturday night and sung together with the congregation on Sunday morning. The words were these:

> Blest be the tie that binds
> Our hearts in Christian love;
> The fellowship of kindred minds
> Is like to that above.

> Before our Father's throne
> We pour our ardent prayers;
> Our fears, our hopes, our aims are one,
> Our comforts and our cares.

> We share each other's woes,
> Each other's burdens bear,
> And often for each other flows
> The sympathizing tear.

> When we are called to part,
> It gives us inward pain;
> But we shall still be joined in heart,
> And hope to meet again.

"The fellowship of kindred minds is like to that above." In the church where the presence of the Holy Spirit is felt there is a foretaste of the future.

CHAPTER 8

Hastening the Day

The dividing line between the old age and the new age is recognized by Christian faith as being at the point of the life of Jesus Christ. He spoke of the signs, which should have been apparent to the people of his day, of the breaking in of the powers of the new age. His followers felt the presence of the Spirit in their hearts and in the church and knew that in Christian love and peace and joy they had a foretaste of the quality of life which would prevail when the kingdom of God was fully come. This "earnest of the Spirit" was, however, only a preliminary down payment. The full possession of what was promised by God was yet to come. The day when his kingdom would be fully established was yet in the future. This much we have established in the preceding chapters of this section, and now we must endeavor to learn more of that great future day toward which biblical expectation is directed, and of the attitude of Christian faith toward it.

What We Look For

The Bible teaches that there it a great day coming. This is called the day of the LORD or the day of God. According

79

to some students of the Bible, the first Bible book which was written in form as we now have it was Amos and the last was 2 Peter. If this is correct, then both the first written book of the Bible and the last have as their main theme the great day of the future. According to the fifth chapter of the book of Amos the expectation of the day of the LORD was widespread at that time among the people of Israel. They evidently anticipated that the coming of the day of the LORD would mean blessing for them quite without regard to the quality of life with which they themselves came to that day. In fact Amos describes very grievous wrongs in the social order of his time and, evidently on account of these things, declares that the day of the LORD which the people so eagerly desired and which they awaited with such smug self-confidence, would be quite the opposite of what they expected:

> Is not the day of the LORD darkness, and not light,
>   and gloom with no brightness in it?
>
> —Amos 5:20

Just because the day of the LORD will mean the overthrow of all evil, however, it will inaugurate the new age of righteousness, and many other of the Old Testament prophets emphasize this positive side of the expectation. Thus in his summary of the prophetic anticipation as a whole, E. F. Scott includes the following as constant features:

For Israel the new age will be one of dominion over the nations and of internal peace and prosperity. The house of David will be restored to its ancient glory. The ten tribes which had disappeared into captivity will return to the mother-land. The oppression of the poor by the rich will come to an end, and princes and judges will rule in righteousness. The world generally will share in the happiness of Israel. Through the chosen people all races of men will be brought to a knowledge of the true God, and will receive His favour and blessing. Wars will entirely cease. The law of God will be obeyed everywhere, and will ensure a universal security and well-being. The blessedness of the new age will be reflected in the world of nature as in human society. Sun and moon will shine with a sevenfold brightness; the earth will yield a more abundant increase; beasts of the forest will lose their fierceness; waste places will blossom into gardens. In that future time all that is sorrowful and unlovely will be done away. Men will turn to God with a changed heart; and will enter upon a new life in a renovated world.[1]

In the later apocalyptic writers we find the same expectation in general, since their work was, as E. F. Scott also points out,[2] in the nature of a commentary upon and deduction from the prophets, but we note as distinctive of their thought an expectation that the new order will come in abruptly by a direct act of God, and a picturing in vivid imagery of many of the details of that happening including the events which precede it and the conditions which accompany it. Concerning this apocalyptic view, Scott writes:

> The first cycle of the world's history is in process of ending, and it cannot end too soon. It has reached the stage of utter exhaustion, and there are no redemptive forces left in it to work out a better future. All that can be hoped for is a fresh beginning—a complete destruction of the old order to make room for the new. It follows that the new order will break in suddenly, and by an act of miracle. . . . The prophets believe that God is working even now for the better time,—overruling the counsels of wicked men and the calamities and even the sins of His people,—in order to fulfil His purposes. The apocalyptists . . . are content to wait on resignedly through the last convulsive throbs of a dying age, to which another will succeed by a sudden miracle.[3]

Finally, in what may be the last book of the Bible to have been written, we find ourselves reading still about the day of the LORD. The Christians have heard Jesus speak about the kingdom of God as at hand. In Christ they have experienced the presence of the powers of the new age. Yet the powers of the old age accomplished his crucifixion,

[1] E. F. Scott, *The Kingdom and the Messiah* (Edinburgh: T. and T. Clark, 1911), pp. 8-9.
[2] *Ibid.*, p. 12.
[3] *Ibid.*, pp. 13-14.

and the expectation of his being present again in splendid fashion seems ever disappointed. Scoffers ask, "'Where is the promise of his coming?'" (2 Peter 3:4) and point out that everything continues just as it was from the beginning of the world. To this the author of 2 Peter replies that it is certain from the word of God that the day of judgment will come. In the unexpectedness of its arrival it will be like a thief. This is probably stated with conscious reminiscence of what Jesus had said, for in his teaching about the future consummation he had used this very figure of speech. In the manner of its coming it will be like a burning up of all existing things. This expectation of a fiery end of the present order was probably a regular feature of apocalyptic thought. In Daniel's vision of the last judgment there is mention of "a stream of fire"; in the Sibylline Oracles it is stated that if men will not repent "then fire shall come upon the whole world";[4] and in the Book of Hymns among the Dead Sea Scrolls there is mention of the raging blaze and the devouring flame at the hour of judgment.[5] Since this passage in the Dead Sea Scrolls speaks of "the foundations of the mountains" being consumed in the fire, it may have been based in part upon Deuteronomy 32:22 where we read in the Song of Moses:

"For a fire is kindled by my anger,
    and it burns to the depths of Sheol,
devours the earth and its increase,
    and sets on fire the foundation of the mountains."

In the Deuteronomic passage, at least, it seems natural to take this language as symbolic rather than literal: God's zealous action against everything that opposes his sovereignty is pictured as like a fire. Whether the similar language of the apocalyptic books was meant literally or

[4] Sibylline Oracles IV, 173.
[5] Gaster, *The Dead Sea Scriptures*, p. 140.

figuratively it is not always easy to tell. Even in the Revelation of John it is often said that what is seen is only "like" the earthly object to which it is compared, and so we are pointed to a greater depth of meaning in the language. In our day, however, when we know that the stars live by the burning of their hydrogen, and when we have an intimation of the prodigious power released in the fusion of hydrogen atoms, it is not too difficult to take literally the prediction of 2 Peter of a day when the elements will melt with fire and what now exists will perish in a great conflagration. This is the statement: "But the day of the Lord will come like a thief, and then the heavens will pass away with a loud noise, and the elements will be dissolved with fire, and the earth and the works that are upon it will be burned up." (2 Peter 3:10.)

What We Cannot Do

It is the anticipation of the Bible, then, that the day of the Lord will assuredly come, a day which will mean the destruction of evil and the establishment in its fullness of the new age. What attitude and action are expected of the Christian in regard to this future day? In 2 Peter immediately following the verse just quoted we find instruction on this matter: "Since all these things are thus to be dissolved, what sort of persons ought you to be in lives of holiness and godliness, waiting for and hastening the coming of the day of God, because of which the heavens will be kindled and dissolved, and the elements will melt with fire! But according to his promise we wait for new heavens and a new earth in which righteousness dwells."

According to this statement the first duty of the Christian is that of "waiting for" the day of God and for the new heavens and new earth which he will bring into being after that which now is is dissolved. The emphasis upon waiting seems to be in line with the outlook of apocalyptic thought as it was noted earlier in this chapter. While some of the apocalypses seem to have been written out of an excessive pessimism, the attitude of waiting in relation to the day of God is in fact necessary because there are some things which we cannot and should not do. Man cannot do God's work. Many of the parables of Jesus remind us that the kingdom comes only through the power of God, a power which is mysterious and mighty. In one of these stories Jesus said, " 'The kingdom of God is as if a man should scatter seed upon the ground, and should sleep and rise night and day, and the seed should sprout and grow, he knows not how. The earth produces of itself, first the blade, then the ear, then the full grain in the ear.' " (Mark 4:26-28.) This is sometimes called the parable of the seed growing secretly, but the emphasis is really not upon secrecy. It may perhaps more accurately be called the parable of the automatic earth. In the original Greek the statement that the earth produces of itself reads literally, "automatically the earth brings forth fruit." This is the truth which is here emphasized. In nature there is a power with which man co-operates but which he does not create and which he does not fully understand. In other words, man can plant a seed but he cannot of himself make it grow, and this, it may be expected, will remain true no matter to what extent scientific knowledge may be extended. There is a mystery here which goes deeper than scientific knowing and doing. A traveler to Japan brought back this saying which had been heard there: "You can tell how many seeds there are in an apple, but no one can tell how many apples there are in a seed." Bulwer-Lytton wrote:

> Whoever plants a seed beneath the sod
> And waits to see it push away the clod—
> He trusts in God.

The process of growth in nature illustrates the process at work in the coming of the kingdom of God. Man waits in trust for a seed to grow; he must wait in trust for God's kingdom to come. The power which is at work and the power which is necessary is more than his own. An Air Force chaplain imprisoned in North Korea for three years tells of how in those dreary days the group of prisoners prayed and felt that God was near. Strangely enough, even their captors began to feel that the prisoners were in touch with a power beyond the human. Most of the group died, some three-fourths of them, and when on one occasion a body was put outside the cell, the captors manifested a superstitious fear as if they believed a power was there which was too much for them. Finally they tried to keep the prisoners from praying, as if they were thereby in touch with a power which no Iron Curtain could ever keep out. There is a power, the power of God and of his kingdom and, since it is greater than his own, it behooves man to wait in trustful dependence upon that power.

Man must also wait for the day of God because he cannot tell God's time. The disciples naturally wished to know when things of which Jesus spoke would happen, and after he predicted the destruction of the temple, they are reported to have asked, "Tell us, when will this be?" It was, however, the flat statement of Jesus that no one knew the time of the end except God. " 'But of that day or that hour no one knows, not even the angels in heaven, nor the Son, but only the Father.'" (Mark 13:32.) His own characteristic way of speaking on this subject was to tell stories which suggested that the coming of the kingdom will be at an unknown and unexpected time. " 'It is like a man going on a journey,'" he said. The man put his servants in charge, but did not tell them when he would return. " 'Watch therefore —for you do not know when the master of the house will come.'" (Mark 13:34-35.) Similarly, in a statement already alluded to earlier in this chapter, Jesus said that "'if the householder had known in what part of the night the thief was coming, he would have watched and would not have let his house be broken into.'" (Matthew 24:43.)

Yet again, we are to wait for the day of God because we should not despise God's patience. It will be remembered that the text we are studying in 2 Peter was written in a time when scoffers were ridiculing the Christians as the adherents of a vain hope. In answer to this attack the writer recalls the statement of the Psalmist that in the sight of God "a thousand years . . . are but as yesterday when it is past" (Psalm 90:4), and himself declares: "With the Lord one day is as a thousand years, and a thousand years as one day." (2 Peter 3:8.) God does not reckon time according to human standards. In fact, moreover, what appears to some as the delay of God in doing what he has said he will do, is really a manifestation of his patience. The lengthened time allows opportunity for all to turn unto him before it is too late. "The Lord is not slow about his promise as some count slowness, but is forbearing toward you, not wishing that any should perish, but that all should reach repentance." (2 Peter 3:9.) The purposes of God are wrought out in great patience. "The trouble is that I'm in a hurry," cried Phillips Brooks, agitated by impatience, "but God isn't." Major things are not often done quickly. Clarence A. Barbour wrote:

God is not defeated; though clouds may be heavy, they will break. If Christianity is a failure there is no hope for men. Nineteen centuries and more have gone, and the kingdom is not established in its fullness. Great things take time. Science asks for millions of years to account for the fashioning of the earth for the habitation of man. Shall we expect man to be fashioned to moral and spiritual perfection in a few hundreds of years? Moral and spiritual changes are more difficult to be reached than material changes. It is harder to fashion a soul than it is to fashion a body. The kingdom which Christ establishes is a kingdom of free men, convinced in mind, moved in heart, definitely committed in will to the good; and that comes slowly.[6]

What We Can Do

Christians are properly described, then, as waiting for the day of God. But they are also described in the passage we are studying as "hastening the coming of the day of God." This suggests that there are things which man can do relative to the coming of the kingdom. A seed, according to the parable of Jesus already cited, grows by a power which exceeds the power or even the comprehension of man. Yet the way it grows depends in part upon the kind of soil in which it is put and the kind of cultivation the soil receives, and these are matters which usually depend upon the action of man. A relatively long story told by Jesus about the sowing of seed, described the seed as falling some along the path where birds devoured it, some on rocky ground where with no depth of soil the sun quickly scorched the young plants, some among thorns by which the growth was choked, and some into good soil where it brought forth manyfold. The interpretation of this parable explains that the seed is the word of the kingdom. Those along the path are the people who hear the word but from whom Satan immediately takes it away. Those on rocky ground are the ones who receive the word with joy but soon fall away in time of tribulation. Those among thorns hear the word but let it be choked by the cares of the world. But those upon good soil are the ones who accept the word and bear fruit in abundance.[7] The kingdom, accordingly, comes to us as the gift and deed of God, but still much depends upon whether and how we

[6] Stanley I. Stuber and Thomas C. Clark, eds., *Treasury of the Christian Faith* (New York: Association Press, 1949), p. 444.

[7] See Mark 4:1-9, 13-20; Matthew 13:1-9, 18-23; Luke 8:4-8, 11-15.

receive and use it. Like a talent or ability, the kingdom cannot be had by wishing for it or demanding it. It is a gift.
But that does not mean there is nothing we can do about
it. Having it, we have a responsibility for what we do
about it. In our own lives we can fritter it away, or bring it
to fruition. As T. Z. Koo has somewhere put it: "The kingdom of God does not exist because of your effort or mine.
It exists because God reigns. Our part is to enter this kingdom and bring our life under his sovereign sway."

Yet the text we are studying in 2 Peter says something
more than we have thus far deduced from it. The statement
is, we remember, that the Christians are "hastening" the
coming of the anticipated day of God. This is the literal
rendering of the original Greek. The idea that what man
does has anything to do with bringing the final consummation sooner than it might otherwise arrive, seems, at least
from some points of view, so daring and even presumptuous
that suggestions have been made for other translations. The
Greek word in question was sometimes used with the connotation of wishing for something, and in accordance with
that idea the American Standard Version renders: "earnestly
desiring the coming of the day of God." The word can also
mean to go in haste, and so the King James Version supplies
the preposition "unto" and reads: "hasting unto the coming
of the day of God." As it stands in 2 Peter, however, the
verb is transitive, that is it expresses an action directed upon
an object, and the object is the "coming" of God's day.
Therefore the indicated rendering seems to be that of the
Revised Standard Version: "hastening the coming of the
day of God." This is a tremendous conception, that the work
of Christians has something to do with when the day of God
comes. Is there really anything we can do to make it come
sooner?

Prayer, according to New Testament teaching, is one such

thing. In fact Jesus explicitly taught his followers to pray, "Thy kingdom come." Unless prayer is an idle exercise, we must believe that earnest utterance of this request will have something to do with the result. It may not be easy to pray this prayer with faith that what is asked will come to pass, but just because discouragement easily besets us, it is important to press the supplication earnestly. Concerning the prayer for the kingdom to come and the will of God to be done on earth as it is in heaven, Rolland W. Schloerb has written:

This prayer is on the lips of thousands of people today. For them it expresses a longing for a world which shall be built in its social relationships upon the principles of justice and love. Not alone in some distant sphere do many modern Christians desire to have God's will done. They would like to see the present world of mankind brought into harmony with the laws of God.

Such a prayer is easily uttered with the lips. It is not so easy to pray it with the faith that it will come to pass. For we live in an age of disillusionment. Many are in doubt with regard to the possibility of building a world which might be called, in the words of Josiah Royce, "a Beloved Community." We thought that we could create a world in which neighborliness would be followed by a spirit of brotherhood. But we are far from the realization of that dream. We are disillusioned.[8]

Preaching, too, is connected with the coming of the kingdom for, according to Mark 13:10, before the end comes "the gospel must first be preached to all nations." The Christion message must be proclaimed everywhere in order for the kingdom to come everywhere. The seed that is the word must be scattered everywhere in order for the fruit to spring up everywhere. So every word and deed which makes known the love of God in Christ for man, speeds the coming of the great day. Pain, too, plays its part in the purchasing of what is hoped for. Of this we will say more in a later

[8] Stuber and Clark, eds., *op. cit.*, pp. 436-437. Used by permission of Mrs. Rolland W. Schloerb.

chapter, but even here we may recall how Paul wrote in prison: "Now I rejoice in my sufferings for your sake, and in my flesh I complete what is lacking in Christ's afflictions for the sake of his body, that is, the church." (Colossians 1: 24.)

It is therefore the part of Christians who look forward to the day of God both to wait for it with patience and to work for it with eagerness. The ages are not too long for God to do his work in, and we must always take the centuries against the hours when we try to see what he is doing. Yet the moment is not too brief to be the time in which some part of his kingdom may come to us, and this may happen even now.

PART THREE:

The Reality of God

CHAPTER 9

Where Is Your God?

Every fresh accomplishment of man offers a possibility for a new expression of human pride. Remarkable as are the achievements which have inaugurated the nuclear-space age, as described earlier in this book, it is not surprising that in some quarters there have been renewed affirmations of the self-sufficiency of man and disparagements of belief in God. As in the days of the Psalmist, so again now men ask the person of faith, "Where is your God?" (Psalm 42:3.) This section of this book will, therefore, be devoted to considering from several approaches relevant to our total inquiry, the reality of God.

Where *Is Your* God?

When the question cited by the Psalmist receives the emphasis on the first word it represents the interrogation of the skeptic. *Where* is your God? This question may imply the observation that God is invisible. Another Psalm contains the same question, and there it is the nations which ask concerning the people of faith, " 'Where is their God?' " (Psalm 115:2.) This Psalm goes on to speak about the idols of the nations, idols made out of silver and gold. To the

93

Psalmist these objects are utterly impotent, but one may readily suppose that the heathen have said in effect, "Look, you can see the representations of our gods! Behold these idols! But where is your God?" The Psalmist answers correctly that these idols which are made by hand can do nothing of themselves. They have mouths, eyes, ears, and noses, but they do not speak or see or hear or smell. They have hands and feet, but they do not feel or walk. As the manufactured products of men, these are assuredly not the true God. But the more sophisticated skeptic, who is quite willing to agree that no visible object can be equated with God, is left to remark all the more emphatically that God is nowhere to be seen. And to such skepticism the answering claim of the Psalmist that "our God is in the heavens" will presumably seem quite irrelevant.

The question, *Where* is your God? may also carry the suggestion that God is inactive. He may be in heaven, but if so, he does nothing on earth. Primitive faith presumably supposes that the gods do everything directly. The falling of a tree, the blowing of the wind, and the flashing of the lightning are the acts of spirits. Modern thought often concludes exactly to the contrary that there is nothing in the universe left for God to do. The so-called laws of nature describe how things work. We know enough of these now to suppose that if we knew all of them, we would understand how everything works. These laws include the laws of chance, which appear to account for the surprising things which happen. Since as many of the surprising things which transpire are bad as good, there is no reason to think that particularly in them God is active. So it often seems as if there were no room left anywhere for God to do anything. Carlyle could remark, "God sits in heaven and does nothing"; and a little boy asked, "What does God do all day?"

In the skeptical question there may also be implied the suggestion that God is impassive. We do not see him, we

do not see him doing anything, and in particular we do not
see him doing anything about the suffering that there is.
He seems to be aloof from it. Yet another Psalm contains
the question, "Where is God?" and connects the interrogation with observation of unrequited wrongs upon earth. This
Psalm was written on an occasion when the heathen had
overrun Jerusalem, and it could have been at the time when
Nebuchadnezzar's armies made their devastating invasion
of Palestine in 586 B.C. Here is the description of what has
happened:

> O God, the heathen have come into thy inheritance;
>   they have defiled thy holy temple;
>   they have laid Jerusalem in ruins.
> They have given the bodies of thy servants
>   to the birds of the air for food,
>   the flesh of thy saints to the beasts of the earth.
> They have poured out their blood like water
>   round about Jerusalem,
>   and there was none to bury them.
>
> —Psalm 79:1-3

Under these circumstances the defeated people of Jerusalem become a taunt to their neighbors. They are made the
object of mocking and derision, for the faith by which they
have lived seems to have been discredited, and the God in
whom they have put their trust appears to have nothing to
do with them. So the Psalmist lifts his lamentation and
utters his plaintive prayer for restoration. "Why," he im-
plores, "should the nations say, 'Where is their God?'"
(Psalm 79:10.) Disaster raises the question of where God is.
A little boy, it is related, once looked for a long time at a
painting of the crucifixion of Christ. Then he said, "If God
had been there, he would not have let them do that." Where
is God when tragedy is present?

"*Where* is your God?" is the question of the skeptic, and

there is probably something of the skeptic, the doubter, the perplexed wonderer, within many of us. The author of the forty-second Psalm, in which we found the first phrasing of our question, was driven to tears by the anguish of his wrestling with this question. He wrote:

> My tears have been my food
> day and night,
> while men say to me continually,
> "Where is your God"
> —Psalm 42:3

He wondered if he would ever see God. "When shall I come and behold the face of God?" he asked. Another Psalm, the twenty-second, begins with an expression of the feeling of forsakenness by God:

> My God, my God, why hast thou forsaken me?
> Why are thou so far from helping me?

These words were quoted by Jesus himself on the cross! Almost everyone, then, may some time or other feel driven to ask the question with which we are dealing. Indeed, perhaps, there may be something not altogether bad in such questioning. If we have never asked any such question it may be because our faith has not been very well thought out; it may be cause we have not yet been very much tested. As a matter of fact the intellectual honesty involved in raising this interrogation may itself sometimes be a sort of faith. As Tennyson said,

> There lives more faith in honest doubt,
> Believe me, than in half the creeds.

Where Is Your God?

Next, let us shift the emphasis to the second word in our question. Where *is* your God? This is now the question of thoughtful faith. Now we are endeavoring to understand and express our faith in relation to the very questions that skepticism raises. In this way of approaching the matter we may say that God is indeed invisible but indicated by what he has made. The Psalmist speaks thus when he says, "The firmament proclaims his handiwork." (Psalm 19:1.) The apostle Paul recognizes the invisibility of God but declares that there are evidences of him in creation. "Ever since the creation of the world his invisible nature . . . has been clearly perceived in the things that have been made." (Romans 1:20.) Augustine has a fine passage in which he asks what it is that he loves when he loves God. This is what he says:

I asked the earth, and it answered me, "I am not he"; and whatsoever things are in it made the same confession. I asked the sea and the deeps, and the creeping things, and they answered me, "We are not thy God; seek above us." I asked the fleeting winds, and the whole air with its inhabitants answered me, "Anaximenes was deceived; I am not God." I asked the heavens, the sun and moon and stars, and they said, "Nor are we the God whom thou seekest." And I replied unto all these, which stand so round about these doors of my flesh, "Answer me concerning my God, since that you are not he, answer me something of him." And they cried out with a loud voice, "He made us." . . . I asked the whole frame of the world concerning my God, and it answered me, "I am not he, but he made me."[1]

Likewise Milton writes:

> These are thy glorious works, Parent of good,
> Almighty, thine this universal frame,
> Thus wondrous fair; thyself how wondrous then!
> Unspeakable, who sitt'st above these heavens,
> To us invisible, or dimly seen
> In these thy lowest works; yet these declare
> Thy goodness beyond thought, and power divine.[2]

[1] *Confessions*, X, vi, 9.
[2] *Paradise Lost*, V.

Where *is* God? Thoughtful faith faces this question and answers with the belief that he is not *in*active but active *in* all things. It is surely a false view of creation to think that God made the world and then left it. The doctrine of creation means rather that God who has made the world also continually sustains it. Without him it would not even exist, for the power of being does not reside in things themselves. Johann Tauler, the Dominican mystic who influenced Luther, stated this truth plainly when he wrote:

> All creatures are absolutely nothing. I do not say that they are small or anything else, but that they are absolutely nothing. That which has no being is nothing. And creatures have no being, because they have their being in God; if God turned away for a moment, they would cease to exist. He who desired to have all the world with God would have nothing more than if he had God alone.[3]

It is surely also a false view of natural law to think that God cannot use it in ways he wishes. The more man learns about the laws of nature the more things he is able to accomplish. Surely these laws, then, are not a prison house for God but rather a manner of his working. Harry Emerson Fosdick has strongly emphasized this fact that knowledge of law is not imprisoning but liberating. He has written: "God is not interned in the concentration camp of his own laws. Granted a real and living God, then all the law-abiding forces of the universe are at his disposal. So, the idea of miracle comes back again, not as broken law, but as law fulfilled."[4] Surely, moreover, there is a vast range of law through which God works which is as yet beyond our knowing. Augustine long ago made an acute comment on this matter when he wrote about remarkable happenings in nature:

[3] *Thirty-Seven Sermons for Festivals*, V. Quoted by John Baillie, *A Diary of Readings* (New York: Charles Scribner's Sons, 1955), 227.

[4] *What Is Vital in Religion* (New York: Harper & Brothers, 1955), p. 17. Used by permission.

We say that all portents are contrary to nature; but they are not so. For how is that contrary to nature which happens by the will of God, since the will of so mighty a Creator is certainly the nature of each created thing? A portent, therefore, happens not contrary to nature, but contrary to what we know as nature.[5]

And yet again it is surely a false view of science itself to think that when we have described a process we have eliminated all mystery. We must not think that God did and does his work only at those points where there are gaps in our knowledge. If we think that, then we will resist the attempts to fill in the gaps, wrongly supposing that with each gap filled in, God is the more pushed out. It must be in the mystery which underlies the whole process, including the parts whose mechanism we have been able to explain as well as the parts where this understanding still eludes us, that God is to be found. Men used to speak, for example, of the "missing link" in evolution, and think that that was where God stepped in. The continuing work of science has now supplied many links which formerly were missing, but it has not dispelled the underlying mystery of the entire process. We used to say that God started life because we did not know how life started. Now there are scientists who think they are in position to speak even on this awesome subject. But notice how a recent statement on this topic comes back before it is finished to include the mystery which cannot be banished by any description no matter how complete. Dr. George Wald, professor of biology at Harvard University, speaking at the annual meeting of the American Association for the Advancement of Science at the end of 1956, was reported as having said:

Our life has a place as part of the order of nature. Life is a part of the physics of our universe. If you start with a universe containing protons, neutrons and electricity, life will eventually appear. It will pursue evolution. And this gives man his place in the universe. He is

[5] *The City of God*, XXI, 8.

its most complex being, the first matter which has begun to contemplate itself.[6]

Whether the first part of the statement is correct or not, we
need not debate, indeed lies only in the purview of scientists themselves. But, however that may be, we cannot fail
to note that with the last sentence we are back again con-
fronting the ultimate mystery. Man is "the first matter which
has begun to contemplate itself." How can matter do that?
Although the entire process is explained by which protons
and neutrons are so arranged that life and self-consciousness
emerge, the self-contemplation that is found in human life
remains itself a mystery. Science may and must trace out
the details of the process, and in what is found there are
elements which it is not unreasonable to believe point us
toward God. But underneath the whole process is a deeper
mystery, and faith receives the revelation which emerges out
of that mystery. Baron Friedrich von Hügel put it like this:

"All Science . . . is essentially the ceaseless seeking, the ceaseless
restating, the ceaseless discovering of error, and the substituting of
something nearer to the truth. I do not see how Science can be asked
to start with a definite God, with a definite Future Life, with anything like a Church; I think it cannot even end with anything more
than a vague reverence and sense of a deep background—a very
elementary Theism will, at best, and can hardly, be reached by it:
such Theism will be, I believe, its maximum. Now, Religion, on the
contrary, begins with a full affirmation of a Reality, of a Reality other
and more than all mankind. It is certain of God, certain of Christ,
certain of the Church. It is a gift from above downwards, not a
groping from below upwards. It is not like Science a coral-reef, it is
more like a golden shower from above. Assimilate Religion to Science,
and you have levelled down to something which, though excellent for
Science, has taken from Religion its entire force and good; you have
shorn Samson of his locks with a vengeance. On the other hand, force
Science up to the level of Religion, or think that you have done so,
and Science affirms far more than, as such, it can affirm, and you, on
your part, are in a world of unreality. . . . For myself I must have both
movements: the palace of my soul must have somehow two lifts—a

[6] Quoted in *The Christian Century*, Jan. 9, 1957, p. 37.

lift which is always going up from below, and a lift which is always going down from above. I must both be seeking and be having. I must both move and repose.[7]

Where *is* God? Thoughtful faith answers once more by saying that God is not impassive but involved in all suffering. This truth may not be demonstrable by logical proof, but it is attested by many facts. We know it to be the testimony of many people that sometimes in loneliness, sorrow, and pain God has seemed closer to them than ever before. We scarcely know why this is; perhaps it is because at such times our guard is down and we are more open to the divine influences. We cannot fail to notice that suffering has often brought redemption. The death of martyrs has given the church an impetus which the works of the living could not give. The crucifixion of Jesus, where it appeared as if God had deserted a man, has since been recognized as the place where in a man God came closest to his whole world.

Where Is Your *God?*

The question we are considering may also be asked with the emphasis on its third word: Where is *your* God? This makes it the question of personal experience. God is indeed invisible, but he is indicated in what he has made, and the question now is simply: can he be felt by us in these things? Alfred Robinson, a graduate of Stanford University and at one time a navy bomber pilot, speaks of the time when his father, Frank B. Robinson, guided him to this feeling. "One of my earliest recollections of dad," he told Marcus Bach, "is the time he took me for a walk into the woods. When we reached a secluded spot he stopped and said, 'Let's be very still. Listen. You can hear the presence of the Almighty.'"[8]

[7] Baron Friedrich von Hügel, *Selected Letters 1896-1924*, ed. by Bernard Holland (London: J. M. Dent and Sons Ltd.; New York: E. P. Dutton and Co., Inc., 1927), pp. 353-354. Used by permission.

[8] Quoted in *The Christian Century*, Jan. 2, 1957, p. 13.

God is not inactive, but active in all things, and the further question is: can he be known by us as a friend? Because of his trust in God, Abraham has been considered to represent the characteristic attitude of the man of faith, and of him it has always been remembered that "he was called the friend of God." God is not impassive, but involved in suffering, and the question now is: can he be known to us as our Father even in times of affliction? It was so with Jesus, and therefore may be with his followers, for even on the cross Jesus called upon the Father.

CHAPTER 10

The Flight from God

In the nuclear-space age, when man is able to set his own moons in the sky and to plan journeys into space, the awareness of his own power and the knowledge that there is no literal heaven a short distance above his head may easily combine to make him ask in its most skeptical emphasis the question reported by the ancient Psalmist, *Where* is God? This we considered in the preceding chapter. Essentially the same matter may be approached also from the point of another passage in the Psalms, where the writer asks,

> Whither shall I go from thy Spirit?
> Or whither shall I flee from thy presence?
> —Psalm 139:7

These questions suggest that men sometimes try to flee from God, and in the words which immediately follow in the same passage we may find some indications of the ways in which that attempt is made.

How We Try to Flee

"If I ascend to heaven," writes the Psalmist. These words can suggest flight from God by human superiority. Early in

103

the Bible we read of men who settled in a plain in the land
of Shinar, and then said, "'Come, let us build ourselves a
city, and a tower with its top in the heavens, and let us make
a name for ourselves.'" (Genesis 11:4.) Since the name
of this tower is said to have been Babel, the reference is
probably to the great staged tower or *ziggurat*, the ruins of
which archeologists have found at ancient Babylon. The
biblical interpretation evidently sees the tower as a sign of
pride. Man thought with this mighty structure to lift himself up to the heavens. He would be equal with God, and if
one is equal with God, one does not need God. If this is the
meaning of the biblical account, it is certainly a symbol of
what has happened many times in human life. When the
accomplishments of technology and of reason are splendid,
pride is often engendered and belief in God seems super-
fluous. Thus in the age of reason, Diderot wrote: "If we go
back to the beginning we shall find that ignorance and fear
created the gods; that fancy, enthusiasm or deceit adorned
or disfigured them; that weakness worships them; that cre-
dulity preserves them; and that custom respects and tyranny
supports them in order to make the blindness of men serve
its own interest." In this fashion theistic belief was explained
away, and man was presumed to occupy a place of such
superiority that faith was unnecessary.

The Psalmist also writes: "If I make my bed in Sheol."
These words suggest flight from God by suicide. In ancient
Israelite belief, Sheol was the shadowy dwelling place of
the dead, therefore to make one's bed in Sheol was to die.
We are not only tempted by our successes to think ourselves
equal with God so that we have no need of him; we are also
tempted by our failures to such despair that we fain would
escape our responsibilities before God by the flight to Sheol.
Paul Tillich says, "I am convinced that there is not one
amongst us who has not at some time desired to be liberated

from the burden of his existence by stepping out of it. And I know that there are some amongst us for whom this longing is a daily temptation."[1]

"If I take the wings of the morning" we read yet again in the Psalm. These words can suggest flight from God by speed. Some of us are hurrying, constantly running, never stopping to think. It is reported that when the passengers on an ocean liner were asked why they were making the trip, half of them replied that they were running away from something. A European observer visited Coney Island, and remarked, "What an unhappy people it must be that turns for happiness here!" Some people think they are handling their drinking all right, then in the face of a difficulty they find this an apparently pleasant escape to which they turn more and more. Running away is a prevalent fashion in the attempted flight from God.

Why It Is Impossible

However, it is the testimony of the Psalmist that flight from God is impossible. The sentences whose beginnings we have quoted thus far, run in full as follows:

> If I ascend to heaven, thou art there!
> If I make my bed in Sheol, thou art there!
> If I take the wings of the morning
>   and dwell in the uttermost parts of the sea,
> even there thy hand shall lead me,
>   and thy right hand shall hold me.
>   —Psalm 139:8-10

It is impossible to flee from God because it is impossible to run away from truth. The truth about man is that, no matter how civilized and sophisticated he becomes; he is

[1] *The Shaking of the Foundations* (New York: Charles Scribner's Sons, 1948), pp. 40-41. Used by permission.

still a creature, beset by evil, and in need of salvation. If the life of modern man is compared with that of the prehistoric cave dweller, it can only be supposed that the commonplaces of today would be utterly unimaginable to our early ancestor. Yet our civilized society with all of its advances is not yet wholly free and happy. We have experienced the worst wars of all time. We are beset by the worst threat of all time. It is as if at the same time that we increase the possibility of good, the potentialities of evil are magnified too. Modern man enjoys the benefits of education, engineering, philosophy, and psychology, yet is still often confused, deluded, and astray. Even in individual life, when we are most successful, we are often most in danger. In Greek tragedy there is a sense of this situation of man. The ancient tragedies, as Tillich points out, picture man essentially thus: "He becomes great and proud and tries to touch the Divine sphere, and he is cast into destruction and despair."[2] Precisely when he tries to flee from God by his own superiority, man finds that he cannot escape the truth of his own creatureliness.

It is not possible to flee from God because it is not possible to escape from existence. Shakespeare's Hamlet ponders death and says:

> To be, or not to be: that is the question. . . .
> . . . To die, to sleep
> . . . 'tis a consummation
> Devoutly to be wished. To die, to sleep;
> To sleep: perchance to dream: ay, there's the rub.[3]

In his own deep assurance of the reality of God, the Psalmist goes beyond this tentative apprehension that death's sleep may not be untroubled by fitful dreams to the affirmation

[2] *Ibid.*, p. 72.
[3] *Hamlet*, Act III, Scene 1.

which seems necessary if we take our faith in God seriously, that even in death we shall still confront him. In the Hebrew this affirmation is, if anything, even more impressive than in the English translation, for it is expressed in an extremely compact form. Indeed Charles A. Briggs supposes, on grounds of the poetic structure, that the original had no verbs at all.[4] If this is the case, the question, "Whither can I go?" was answered simply: "If to heaven, there thou; if to Sheol, behold!" It is, of course, correct to supply in English translation the words which are simply understood in the Hebrew, and to render the statement as the American Standard Version does, for example, "behold, thou art there." But the short form of the original Hebrew is very striking: "if to Sheol, behold!" Even there, behold God! So even there one has not fled from him.

It is impossible to flee from God because it is impossible to run away from oneself. A famous man said that he went to Italy to get away from himself, but when he arrived in Italy, he found that he was there himself. Though we hurry to the uttermost parts of the earth, upon arrival we are there ourselves, there with our past, our problems, our perplexities, and our inward confrontation with God. As the poet wrote:

> Our pleasures come from cars and planes
> As changeable as weather vanes;
> But in ourselves, for more or less
> Lies all that brings us happiness.[5]

We Cannot Get Lost

If, then, it is impossible to flee from God, we may be assured that it is also impossible to get lost from him, given

[4] *The Book of Psalms,* in The International Critical Commentary (New York: Charles Scribner's Sons), II (1907), p. 494.

[5] Lalia Mitchell Thornton, "Difference," in *The Christian-Evangelist,* Apr. 25, 1956, p. 422. Used by permission.

only man's willingness to place his trust in him. As a matter of fact, this is in all probability the great truth which the Psalmist intends to emphasize. Thus far we have used his words to illustrate our own all-too-frequent attempts to run away from God, and there are some commentators who think that the Psalmist himself was contemplating the possibility of escape from God. In the tenth verse, however, where he thinks of being in some very distant part of the sea, and affirms,

> even there thy hand shall lead me,
> and thy right hand shall hold me,

it is plain that he is thinking of the presence of God, not as something to fear and try to flee from, but as something to be grateful for and to rejoice in. Thus the entire passage about the inescapable omnipresence of God may most probably be taken as saying in effect, "There is no place I could go where I should lose his kindly presence and helpful power."[6]

God is in the heights. The indomitable Sherpa, Tenzing, was one of the two men who were the first ever to stand on the top of Mount Everest, highest known mountain on earth. Tenzing is a Buddhist, of course, but a man whose humble faith makes him akin to men of faith in all the world. Of his experience on the summit of Everest he has said: "What I felt was a great closeness to God, and that was enough for me. In my deepest heart I thanked God. And as we turned to leave the summit I prayed to Him for something very real and very practical: that, having given us our victory, he would get us down off the mountain alive."[7]

[6] Harold L. Creager and Herbert C. Alleman in *Old Testament Commentary*, ed. by Herbert C. Alleman and Elmer E. Flack (Philadelphia: The Muhlenberg Press, 1948), p. 591.

[7] Tenzing Norgay and James Ramsey Ullman, *Tiger of the Snows* (New York: G. P. Putnam's Sons, 1955), p. 252. Used by permission.

During the battle of Britain a young fighter pilot, John Magee, served with the Royal Air Force and was killed in an aerial accident. Before his death he wrote a poem in which he expressed his sense of exhiliration in flight and spoke, in poetic way, of putting out his hand and touching the face of God. In his own book, *God Is My Co-Pilot,* Colonel Robert L. Scott, Jr., tells of how against the noise of his airplane engine he has heard his voice repeating the words which Magee wrote.[8] Man will not go into any heights of space where God is not present.

God is in the depths. A minister was driving his automobile when it was struck from the left side and virtually demolished. He went to the hospital with multiple broken bones, and was at the brink of death at least three times. Prior to this event he had feared death and, although it was a regular part of his work, the conduct of funerals had been an ordeal in which sometimes he was almost paralyzed with fear. Writing after his accident he says:

Now that I have gone down to the brink and looked death full in the face, I find it is not to be feared. As a matter of fact during those first few days there were times when *death* looked more like a friend than *life*. I feel sure that my experience will release me from those fears that were hindering my ministry. If it does, my trip to the brink and back will be one of the most profitable experiences of my life.[9]

One recalls the words of Donald Hankey, wounded and dying on the battlefield: "God! God everywhere—and underneath, the everlasting arms."

God is there, whether near or far. In his remarkable book entitled *I Have Seen God Do It,* Sherwood Eddy witnesses to his recognition of the work of God in America, Great

[8] Hermann Hagedorn, *Sunward I've Climbed, The Story of John Magee, Poet and Soldier, 1922-1941* (New York: The Macmillan Company, 1942), p. 7; Robert L. Scott, Jr., *God Is My Co-Pilot* (New York: Charles Scribner's Sons, 1943), p. 277.

[9] W. M. W., "Back From the Brink," in *The Christian-Evangelist,* Apr. 4, 1956, p. 351. Used by permission.

Britain, Czechoslovakia, Russia, China, India, Japan, the Philippines, and elsewhere around the world. In Russia he received a letter from a medical student who, lacking all faith, had said good-by to her roommate and was going to the river to end her life. On the way she saw a notice of Dr. Eddy's meeting with the subject, "The Meaning of Life." Afterward she wrote this letter:

"I am a medical student troubled by doubts and passions. I had lost all faith and saw no meaning in life. I decided to put an end to my days by suicide. Once I loved God, in my infant recollections. Formerly he always helped me, but afterwards all went downwards in my life. I ceased to pray and to believe in him. Day and night I thought of committing suicide. I considered it to be cowardly but could not conquer myself. I gave up books and study. Daily a friend came to see me, but being an unbeliever too, could not tell me anything that I could not have told myself. On the 25th of January I left her for the last time, saying: 'Good-bye; tomorrow I will cease to exist.' A life without meaning, without aim, without eternity, with nothing but human pleasures, was disgusting to me. It was then that I saw the notice of your lectures on *The Meaning of Life, A Rational Basis for Religion*, etc. I went, and on returning, I went to sleep for the first time during the last two months without thought of suicide. Since then I have attended all your lectures. I now read the Bible daily and am again able to pray. I do not know what the future will be, but now I desire again to live. In any case, I shall prolong my life for the next three months to make the test of Jesus Christ by reading the Gospels once more and making the experiment which you suggested. Pray for me."[10]

From this and many other experiences it was the conclusion of Dr. Eddy "that God cannot be proved but that he can be known."

We cannot flee from God; we also cannot get lost from him, provided only we are willing to place our trust in him.

[10] Sherwood Eddy, *I Have Seen God Do It* (New York: Harper & Brothers, 2d ed. 1940), p. 57. Used by permission.

CHAPTER 11

The Greatness of God[1]

In the nuclear-space age man has made remarkable new achievements, but man is still man and accordingly still dependent upon God and in need of God. This we have been saying in the preceding chapters. The age of the atom and of space also means vastly expanded horizons for man, as we have likewise seen, and it is therefore also important to notice that the biblical doctrine of God speaks of him in terms of such greatness that the most far-flung universe conceivable lies still, as it were, in the hollow of his hand. In the Old Testament we have found an impressive statement of the omnipresence of God in Psalm 139, a Psalm which also speaks plainly of the omniscience of God. Turning now to the New Testament, we also find a remarkable statement of the greatness of God in James 1:17. In the King James Version this verse reads: "Every good gift and every perfect gift is from above, and cometh down from the Father of lights, with whom is no variableness, neither shadow of turning."

[1] This chapter appeared originally in *The Pulpit*, XXIV, 1, Jan. 1953, pp. 9-11, and is reproduced here with adaptations. Copyrighted by the Christian Century Foundation and reprinted by permission of *The Pulpit* from the issue of January, 1953.

In working out something of what this verse suggests about the nature of God, use will be made of some items of scientific knowledge, and to show that this is appropriate and even necessary we may recall that there was already no small accumulation of such knowledge in the ancient world. As we have seen, both a conception of the atomic structure of things and a hope that man could go near to the heavenly bodies existed in ancient times. Speaking of science in general, both Dampier in his *History of Science*[2] and Sarton in his *Introduction to the History of Science*[3] begin the story of science many thousands of years ago. In Babylonia a large number of texts have been found from the time of Hammurabi, about 1700 B.C., in the fields of medicine, chemistry, geology, botany, mathematics, and astronomy. In Babylonia, Egypt, and the Hellenistic world, the knowledge of mathematics and astronomy was particularly advanced, as Neugebauer shows in detail in *The Exact Sciences in Antiquity*.[4] In mathematics the Babylonians, for example, possessed the multiplication table and tables of squares and cubes. They calculated according to the decimal system, in which reckoning is by tens, but they also employed duodecimal and sexagesimal systems, in which reckoning was by twelves and by sixties respectively.

In astronomy we have already noted that the sun, moon, and five planets were well known, and the days of the week were named after these seven heavenly bodies. The month was recognized as it was determined by the phases of the moon. The path of the sun among the stars was known, and

[2] William C. Dampier, *A History of Science* (Cambridge: University Press; New York: The Macmillan Company; 3d ed. 1943).

[3] George Sarton, *Introduction to the History of Science* (Baltimore: Published for the Carnegie Institution of Washington, by The Williams & Wilkins Company, 3 vols. 1927-47).

[4] O. Neugebauer, *The Exact Sciences in Antiquity* (Princeton: Princeton University Press, 1952).

the regions of the sky were divided into the signs of the zodiac. The lunar and the solar year were known and it was understood that the twelve lunar months, of twenty-nine or thirty days each, made a year shorter than the solar year. In Babylonia the discrepancy was rectified by intercalating into the lunar calendar seven additional months in every nineteen years, a system which accomplished the necessary adjustment with a theoretical error of only two hours, four minutes, and twenty-five seconds in the nineteen years. In Egypt it was recognized that the calendar year caught up with the true year once in a Sothic cycle of 1,460 years, which means that the ancient Egyptians computed the true year at 365.25 days, whereas modern astronomers make it 365.2422. The relative motions of the sun and moon were charted and, at least by the sixth century B.C., eclipses were predicted.

Interestingly enough, in the recently discovered Dead Sea Scrolls we find that the Qumran community which wrote these manuscripts was much interested in the sun, moon, and stars, and we gather that they adhered to a calendar of a remarkable sort in which a given calendar date fell always on the same day of the week, an arrangement which is not true even in our calendar today. It is also of interest to note that there are a number of similarities between the Dead Sea Scrolls and the letter of James, indicating the possibility of connection between the Qumran community and James.[5] We proceed, then, to the study of the text in James with the realization that it was written at a time when considerable scientific knowledge was available, and with the hope that in the study we may be guided in our own thought about the relationship of God to the scientifically known universe.

[5] Gaster, *The Dead Sea Scriptures*, pp. 15-17.

The Father of Lights

The first part of the statement of James is relatively familiar and we may pass directly to the last part in which three things are said about the nature of God. The first is that God is the Father of lights. This teaches us that God is the creator of the universe. This is a truth to which the entire Bible bears witness, and with which we have already been concerned either explicitly or implicitly in much of the present book. It is an insight to which at least not a few leaders of modern science and philosophy themselves seem inclined to return. Leslie Paul, to cite at this point but a single example, writes: "From a metaphysical examination . . . of certain important aspects of modern knowledge one may arrive without straining the evidence at the notion of a creative God. . . . Quite simply one may say then that it is rather more rational to believe in God than not to believe."[6]

No Variableness

In the second place, the statement of James declares that with God is no variableness. The word translated "variableness" in the King James Version may also be rendered "variation" as in the Revised Standard Version, or "change" as in the translation by James Moffatt. It has the sense of alternation, of passing from one hand to the other, or from one side to the other. Looked at carefully in the original, it is at once recognizable as the Greek root from which we derive the word "parallax."

This word is frequently employed by astronomers, physicists, and even amateur photographers. The "parallax" is the apparent displacement of an object when seen from two different points of view. If we hold two objects in a line

[6] *The Meaning of Human Existence* (Philadelphia and New York: J. B. Lippincott Co., 1950), p. 103. Used by permission.

in front of our face and look at them, first with the left eye
and then with the right, they seem to move in relation to
each other. In stereoscopic photography two cameras are
used, taking two pictures, each from its own angle; thus
depth is recorded. In astronomy the same principle is uti-
lized in order to measure the distance of a star. When the
earth is on one side of its orbit around the sun, the angle of
direction to the star is noted. When the earth is on the far
side of its orbit, six months later, the same star is looked at.
It appears to be in a slightly different place. Knowing the
two angles and the distance between the two points of view,
it is possible to calculate the distance of the star. Parallax in-
volves an apparent displacement when things are seen from
two different points of view.

We human beings are all involved in parallax when we
look at things, because we look at them from our particular
point of view. But our text tells us that with God there is
no parallax. God is not restricted to a particular point of
view from which he sees things in a partial and one-sided
way. With him is no parallax. Let us explore this conception
in two realms, space and time.

We are all in particular places, and we are all limited
by the places which we occupy. We occupy the place of a
coal miner. As a coal miner we see things from that point
of view. We remember dingy towns, a dark, dank, dangerous underground, and all the lives that have been lost and
all the protection that has not been given. Or we occupy
the place and the point of view of the employer, and here
we see the economic picture differently. We are concerned
for full production. We believe that life can be abundant
for everybody only if everybody works hard all the time.
Here are two different points of view, and sometimes the
person in the one spot cannot see how things look to the
person in the other.

Again, we may experience the difference between Jew and Gentile. As a Jew, we have been persecuted many times, we have had to fight and struggle to succeed. As a Gentile, we may have had one unfortunate experience with a person of the other faith, and have generalized that into a complete dislike of all those of the other religion. Or also it may be that since Russia occupies one place and America another, a Russian may see things from one point of view and an American from another. God, however, is not limited to any one of these partial viewpoints. There is no parallax with him. He sees the entire picture. God can see the case of both the laborer and the employer, of both the Jew and the Gentile, of both the Russian and the American.

Therefore, if a person is to live as a child of God—if a person is to do what Jesus talked about, to seek to be perfect as the heavenly Father is perfect—then he must endeavor to overcome, as far as he can, the limitations of his own partial viewpoint. As far as possible, he must rise above the prejudices of partiality. In that we have the help and guidance of Jesus himself. As the representative of the infinite wisdom of God, Jesus transcended limited, partial points of view. In his day, Jews and Samaritans could not understand one another. Though Jesus was by birth a member of the Jewish group, he went through Samaria; he dealt kindly with Samaritans; and he made a good Samaritan the hero of one of the greatest stories he ever told.

Now about the matter of time. Is our text telling us that there is also no parallax with God in respect to time? Einstein has taught us that there is relativity not only in space but also in time. Two events take place in time, one prior to the other, from our point of view. A precedes B. But from the point of view of another observer, conceivably B may precede A. If our text is telling us that with God there is no parallax of time, then God sees all events not as past, present, and future as we see them from our point of view, nor in the reverse order in which another finite observer might see them; but from his infinite point of view, God sees past, present, and future as all in an eternal present.

Here, then, we are called to overcome the tyranny of time. Leslie Weatherhead remarks: "An obsession with years spoils our perspective." He describes the men of the Old Testament, whose chief desire seems to have been to live a long time. They wished to see the outworking of God's salvation and they hoped they would live long enough to do so, but they never did and so for the most part they died discouraged. Weatherhead says,

What an amazing difference there is in the men of the New Testament! They are certain of immortal life. Time is merely a deceiver. Life went on, and it was gain to be without a body and away from earth and uncramped by time. There was no such thing as loss of life. There cannot be loss of life. Life goes on in another room. There is only a passing from one room to another, or perhaps it is more like going out of a stuffy room into the open air of the moors and mountains. . . . Time cannot steal anything vital, cannot hurt or destroy. It is an opportunity to be used, a room to be lived in, a university from which to graduate; but the spirit of man belongs to another category, and his life is in the eternal.[7]

None of us human beings can get completely out of the space that we occupy, but we can try by God's help to see the place that the other person occupies, and get a little above the prejudices of our customary partiality. None of us by just wishing to can step outside the room of time, but we can so live in the room of time that we see it surrounded by the eternity of God, from whose great perspective many of the things that happen within time must seem different and far better, and we may overcome somewhat thereby the tyranny of time.

[7] Leslie D. Weatherhead, *The Significance of Silence* (New York and Nashville: Abington Press, 1945), pp. 173-174, 176. Used by permission.

No Shadow of Turning

The third statement of our text is that there is no shadow of turning with God. This teaches us that God is everlastingly faithful. Turning is what casts shadows. It is because the earth is turning that the sun goes down and the shadows of the evening are spread out. Stand on the top of a high mountain at sunset and watch the shadow of the mountain race eastward across the plain: the earth is turning—thence comes the shadow. The sun and the moon and the earth are turning in relation to each other, and these respective revolutions sometimes work together to produce eclipses. This is the shadow of turning of which the text is speaking.

Translated into life, this is the dark shadow that is cast by the changeableness of faithless men. The leader of a nation is faithless to his pledged word, a person entrusted with a responsible task fails to carry it out, one who has taken a solemn vow goes back on it—all these things cast dark shadows. Over against this is the steadfastness of a true friend, whom you can trust absolutely, no matter what happens. In the Old Testament consider the examples of Saul, Jonathan, and David. In his madness and melancholia, Saul turned faithlessly from approval of David to attempts upon his life. Against that dark background, the true friendship of Jonathan and David, faithful to each other in all circumstances, shone more brightly. God, then, is like a most faithful friend and more, always there, always to be depended upon. In the New Testament it says that even if we are faithless, he remains faithful, because he cannot deny himself.

God is the Father of lights. Therefore he is the creator of this universe and our maker. With him is no variableness. Therefore he can help us to overcome the prejudices of partiality and the tyranny of time. With him is no shadow

of turning. He can help us to be more steadfast and faithful.

It is indeed a great God who is described in our text. In
his greatness we may find rest and strength. Sidney Lanier
has put it like this in his poem, "The Marshes of Glynn":

> As the marsh-hen secretly builds on the watery sod,
> Behold I will build me a nest on the greatness of
>   God:
> I will fly in the greatness of God as the marsh-hen
>   flies
> In the freedom that fills all the space 'twixt the
>   marsh and the skies:
> By so many roots as the marsh-grass sends in the
>   sod
> I will heartily lay me a-hold on the greatness of
>   God.

CHAPTER 12

Too Good to Be True?[1]

Because of the nature of our present study in which we are endeavoring to understand the reality of God in relation to the universe of the atom and of space, we have laid most emphasis upon the facts, as set forth in biblical doctrine, that God is the creator of the world, that he knows it in all its detail, and that he is present in it in all its vast reaches. But we have also seen that the Bible envisions a cosmic redemption as being in the purpose of God, and so we must not fail to set forth something of the personal relationship of God to the persons whom he would redeem. To give a brief outline of this relationship in terms of the message found in the New Testament about God's loving kindness toward men is the purpose of the present chapter.

In the New Testament the name for the Christian message is "gospel." The Greeks had a word, from which our word "angel" is derived, which meant "to bring news." To that they added a prefix to make a term signifying "to bring good news." From this comes our verb "evangelize." Related

[1] This chapter appeared originally in *The Pulpit*, XXVIII, 3, March 1957, pp. 7-9, and is reproduced here with adaptations. Copyrighted by the Christian Century Foundation and reprinted by permission of *The Pulpit* from the issue of March, 1957.

to this verb was a Greek noun which we translate "evangel" or "gospel." It meant the crown which they put on the head of a runner who burst in with good news from a distant place. Or it meant the sacrifice which they offered in thanksgiving when they received good news. Or it meant the good news itself. That is the word which is used in the New Testament for the Christian message.

It is a wonderful thing to receive good news. When we do, how delighted we are! Whether it comes as a telegram, a telephone call, or a letter, or more directly as somebody comes to us with good news, we are happy to get it. It is also a wonderful thing to take good news to somebody. It is a privilege to go to others and tell them something good. You see the light break on their faces. How happy they are! This is the way it is in the New Testament when the Christian message is brought. In the Gospel according to Mark, we read of Jesus, that he came preaching the gospel of God, that is the good news about God and from God. Later we read in the same Gospel that "the great throng heard him gladly." In Acts we read how Paul and his companions came to the city of Antioch. They stood up there and said, "We bring you the good news." A little later we read, "When the Gentiles heard this, they were glad."

It seems a tragedy that sometimes evangelism has come to signify threatening people. Indeed, we ought to stand in horror and dread of sin and its penalties, but the Christian message is primarily about how to experience the victory. It seems regrettable also when the message is only one of admonition to duty, exhortation to responsibility. That also is getting the matter backwards. The Christian message is, first of all, wonderfully good news. When we have heard it, then, because we are grateful, we want to do the various things that are our duty and responsibility.

Now let us glance through the New Testament, and bring

together several of the statements in which there is this sense that what is told is something very good, almost incredibly good, almost too good to be true! Yet, actually, it is too good not to be true, and too true not to be good.

What God Has Done

The first fact that we may notice is the amazing friendliness of what God has already done for us. About this, John says that God loved us before we loved him. "We love, because he first loved us." As we try to understand this for ourselves, we remember that Jesus took illustrations from the home and family life and used them as pictures of God and man. We come, then, into a family as a tiny baby, helpless, with little understanding. But we are received in the ordinary home with love, and surrounded and sustained by love. The mother has prepared a crib and soft blankets. The father is out at work to earn money to pay the bills. The baby instinctively thrives on this love; it languishes if it is lacking. The baby is not yet old enough to understand, to comprehend. Eventually we grow up enough to realize what our parents have done for us. Then we become aware that they loved us before we were mature enough to know very much about what they were doing for us, to comprehend their love, or adequately to reciprocate it. Perhaps it is a long time in life before we fully realize what our dear parents have done for us, and then we love them the more because they have loved us already. Even so God has put us here in this world and prepared a thousand things in it to make it home for us. We gradually become aware that his love has been around us even before we were understanding enough to know it, before we comprehended him. It is said that when it became possible to communicate with Helen Keller, she was told about God. She signed back, "I have always known him, but I did not know his name." Even before we know God's name, his love is around us. He loved us before we loved him. We grow up and learn to answer his love with our love.

Another part of this amazing friendliness of God toward us is that he showed that love in the fact that Christ died for us while we were yet sinners. Paul talks about this with the feeling that it is almost too good to be true, something almost incredibly wonderful. Paul thinks of a righteous man, probably meaning a rather stern, harsh man. One would scarcely die for such a person. Then there is a good man, a lovable man. Perhaps somebody will die for him. But Christ's sacrifice, says Paul, depended on no such worthiness on our part. We were yet sinners when he died for us. (Romans 5:7-8.) We were those who snarled at him at the foot of the cross. We were those who followed afar off. We were those who denied, betrayed, were little interested—and he died for us while we were yet of such sort. This shows us what God is like. We see, then, an amazing friendliness in God toward us.

What God Offers

In the second place we notice an amazing generosity in God's offer to us, in the conditions of salvation. For one thing, God offers us forgiveness if we will only repent. Here are several passages in the Old Testament and the New which state this: Isaiah 55:7—"Let the wicked forsake his way, and the unrighteous man his thoughts; let him return to the Lord, that he may have mercy on him, and to our God, for he will abundantly pardon." Ezekiel 33:14-15—"Though I say to the wicked, 'You shall surely die,' yet if he turns from his sin and does what is lawful and right . . . he shall surely live." Luke 24:47, summing up the message of Christianity—"That repentance and forgiveness of sins should be preached in his name to all nations." 1 John 1:9

—"If we confess our sins, he is faithful and just, and will forgive our sins and cleanse us from all unrighteousness."

This is so good that people can almost not believe it. The proof that people can hardly believe it may be seen in such a thing as the institution of penance in the Middle Ages. At that time a vast penitential system was set up by men who could not believe the words of the Bible as they stand. In this system it was necessary for the priest to pronounce absolution. This was believed to give freedom from eternal punishment, but temporal punishment still had to be undergone by the sinner, either in this life or in purgatory. Catalogues were therefore made of the penances which should be performed to make up for sins. In these catalogues all the different kinds of evildoing were listed, and the corresponding things were specified which man must do to make up for the wrongs committed. For one sin a man must stay up all night and pray. For another he must make a visit to a holy place. For yet another he must go on pilgrimage for ten years; or instead, if he chose, pay a certain sum of money. This was the most dangerous part of the system. Forgiveness, it seemed, might be purchased by paying money.

Indulgences were offered for sale so that those who had sinned might buy a ticket which would set them free. At one time in particular, Pope Leo X was interested in obtaining more money for work on St. Peter's Church in Rome, and Albert of Brandenburg, the Archbishop of Mainz, needed more money to pay back the loan with which he had purchased his office, and so indulgences were being sold. John Tetzel was peddling them in one part of Germany. Here is an eyewitness' account of the arrival of Tetzel in a German town:

When the indulgence-seller approached the town, the document proclaiming the indulgence was carried before him on a cloth of velvet and gold, and all the priests and monks, the town council, the schoolmasters and their scholars, and all the men and women went out to meet him with banners and candles and songs, forming a great procession; then, all the bells ringing and all the organs playing, they accompanied him to the principal church; a red cross was set up in the midst of the church, and the pope's banner was displayed; in short, one might think they were receiving God himself.[2]

Then the indulgence-seller preached a sermon, in which he declared that "the gate of heaven was open" and that the sale would begin. And people came and paid their money to buy indulgences which would take care of their sins. They could not believe that it was as simple as it says in the New Testament. This was, of course, when Martin Luther posted his theses, in which he declared, "The Christian who has true repentance has already received pardon from God altogether apart from an indulgence, and does not need one; Christ demands this true repentance from every one." That is the true teaching of the Christian religion.

This is the easiest thing in the world: all you have to do is repent. It is also the hardest thing in the world, for you must turn with all your heart to God. If the matter were to be settled on the basis of indulgences, then you could commit a sin, and buy an indulgence and take care of it. You could commit another sin if you wanted to, and buy another indulgence to make up for it, just as you collect parking tickets down town. You can get another one and take care of it too whenever necessary. So what the Bible offers is harder than that, and yet it is easier than that. Nothing is required but our turning to God, and then, it is promised, we shall be forgiven.

Consider also the amazing generosity of God's offer when we are told in the New Testament that we may be justified by faith. According to legalism, whether in parts of the Old

[2] Frederick Mecum (Myconius), quoted by Thomas M. Lindsay, *A History of the Reformation* (New York: Charles Scribner's Sons, 1928), I, p. 213.

Testament or elsewhere, it is necessary to build up our own good works in the sight of God, to be considered right. If we break as much as one law, we are guilty of all. According to some medieval doctrine, salvation is a quantitative thing. So many good works must be wrought in order to attain salvation before God. But according to Paul, and according to Martin Luther, and according to God's authentic word through these great messengers of his, we may be justified by faith. If we have loving trust in God, he will account us as right in his sight on the basis of that faith. Paul Tillich often says: "Faith is courage to accept the fact that we are accepted by God, even though we are unacceptable." Here is the amazing generosity of God's offer to us. It is almost too good to be true. People have not been able to believe it, but it is too good not to be true.

What God Promises

In the third place, beyond the amazing friendliness of what God has done for us already, and the amazing generosity of what he offers to us right now, we note the amazing blessedness of what he promises for the future.

He promises that death will be a door and heaven will be home. "In my Father's house are many rooms." We walk across the room of a great house, and on the far side of the room in which we have been, there is a doorway, and it opens into another room. This is the amazing blessedness of the promise that is ours, that when we come to death, we shall pass "through an open door." In the words which are used with the largo of the *New World Symphony,* "I'm agoin' home . . . jes goin' home . . . through an open door."

A minister came back recently from abroad and related an incident of which he had heard in Great Britain. A scrub-woman in London was taken sick. Her friends made it possible for her to go to the hospital. While she was convalescing there, she went up and down the corridor and became acquainted with other patients. Across the hall from her was a boy, twelve years old, redheaded, freckle-faced. She and he talked every day. Then one morning she was wakened early by commotion in the hall, and before long the boy's mother came in to tell her, "The doctors say Johnny has about ten minutes to live. Won't you say something to him?" That was a hard assignment. But this London scrubwoman, with the courage of a great Christian, walked quietly across the hall and sat down beside Johnny. She took his thin hand between her calloused palms and looked at him and said: "Listen, Johnny, God made you. God loves you. God sent his Son to save you. God wants you to come home to live with him." The little boy propped himself up on his elbows, feebly, and entreated his friend, "Say it again." Quietly, she repeated the same words: "God made you. God loves you. God sent his Son to save you. God wants you to come home to live with him." Johnny looked into the calm face of his friend and said, "Tell God, 'Thank you.'"

It is appropriate for us to tell God "thank you" for loving us before we ever loved him; for letting Jesus Christ die for us when we were yet sinners; for promising us forgiveness if we will only repent; for promising us that he will look upon us as all right in his sight if we have faith and trust him; for promising us that when we come to death, it will be a door, and that heaven will be home.

PART FOUR:

The Christian Imperative

CHAPTER 13

The World Responsibility of Christians

In the first section of this book we described the new age in which we live, an age which is at once amazing and frightening, the nuclear-space age. In the second section we endeavored to understand the even more important new age in which the Christian lives, the age of the beginning of the kingdom of God, which began with Jesus Christ. In the third section we traced biblical teachings concerning the omnipotence, omniscience, omnipresence, and loving kindness of God, and saw that the world of the atom and of space, tremendous and even terrifying as it is, is still his world. In this fourth section we must now consider the imperative which devolves upon Christians today. Since it is a day when the Sputniks are circling the earth it is a time for renewed emphasis upon the world responsibility of Christians.

This world responsibility is plainly enunciated in the New Testament. For a single striking statement of it we may recall the words found in Matthew 13:38: "The field is the world." Jesus had told the story of the sower, and

131

these words are found in the following explanation of that parable. The sower of the seed, it is explained, is the Son of man, that is the One who brings the kingdom; the field of his work is the world. Those who are concerned with the kingdom of God must, therefore, be concerned with the whole world.

The field of God's interest is not less than the world. Each people upon earth has naturally tended to think of itself as at the center. It is said that the Shah of Persia retains the title, "The Center of the Universe." In Burma a palace at Mandalay has the inscription, "Now we are at the center of the world." The Chinese called theirs the Middle Kingdom. Japanese mythology states that the Japanese islands were the first things created. And in the United States of America we have often enough thought of our land as having the central place in world affairs. But when the New Testament declares that "God . . . loved the world" it uses a word which is literally *cosmos* and can certainly be restricted to no single area upon earth, no matter how favored or strategic.

The field of Christ's concern is nothing less than the world. Jesus seemed always interested in every individual person, in a way that transcended race, creed, or nationality. He was interested in the Syrophoenician woman, the Good Samaritan, and the Roman centurion. He dealt with these individually, evidently considering each one precious and priceless in the sight of his heavenly Father.

The field to which truth applies is also the whole world. In some matters there is great variation from place to place upon the earth. Habits and customs differ in different parts of the world, and the world is doubtless more interesting because of this variety. But in other realms, if a thing is true it has to be true everywhere. If the law of gravity correctly describes the way two particles, free to move, are accelerated toward each other in proportion to the product of their masses and in inverse proportion to the square of the distance between them, then this description is valid not only in the United States of America but also in Africa and Asia. In the moral and spiritual realm there presumably is room for variety in habit and custom but, at a deeper level, fundamental truth must exist which is equally applicable everywhere on earth. Of such truth we may say that only if it is valid for every man, is it valid for any man. In relation to such truth, the field is the world.

Compassion

The Christian, therefore, who knows of the love of God and the concern of Christ for the whole world, and of the relevance of the truth of the gospel to the whole world, must necessarily have a world responsibility. For one thing, he will answer the needs of the world with deeds of compassion. According to Exodus 3:9-10 God said to Moses: " 'And now, behold, the cry of the people of Israel has come to me, and I have seen the oppression with which the Egyptians oppress them. Come, I will send you to Pharaoh that you may bring forth my people, the sons of Israel, out of Egypt.' " The children of Israel were at that time a displaced and oppressed people. Although the Pharaoh under whom they suffered is not named, we note that for him they build a store-city named Raamses and therefore we suppose that he must have been the famous ruler of that name, Ramses II. This Egyptian ruler, who was probably on the throne soon after 1300 B.C., is well known to us as a great conqueror and a great builder. If his heel was upon the children of Israel, they were indeed in a sad plight. But the cry of the people was heard by God, and God summoned Moses to hear too and to act.

"I hear my people crying. . . . Whom shall I send . . .?"

writes the poet in expression of God's word today.[1] The cry of many of God's children rises today because they are hungry. During World War II some persons underwent experiments in controlled starvation. They told afterward how more and more they became literally obsessed by the thought of food. They could think, talk, and dream of nothing else. It is conservatively estimated that one-third of the world is hungry today. In India a widow throws herself under a train because she cannot stand any longer to hear her children wailing for food. In her book *Hunger and Hope*, Rowena Ferguson says:

People, first of all, must have bread. They must possess the means of physical survival before any knowledge of "life's meaning" can take hold. In fact, without bread men are incapable of making sound decisions. In order to survive, they will give up the other good things of life. History is full of instances when hungry people in a choice between bread and freedom have chosen bread.[2]

The cry of the homeless still arises in our world. The problem of the refugee has been called "the largest single human issue facing the world today." A refugee has been defined as anyone who has been uprooted from home, has crossed a frontier, and looks for help to a government other than his former one. By this definition, between 1945 and 1957, 40,000,000 people became refugees, and at the end of 1957 over 16,000,000 were reported as still in need of help, 6,050,000 in Europe, 1,350,000 in the Middle East, 5,000,000 in Southeast Asia, and 4,000,000 in the Far East. One displaced person in Europe wrote a letter in which he said on behalf of himself and the others in his camp:

We are hard working people who do not easily give up when faced with hardships. The present life we live is a miserable and hopeless vegetation, but we are proud to say we do not pass our time in idleness. . . . We are people who have lost everything, even our beloved

[1] John Haynes Holmes, "The Voice of God Is Calling."
[2] New York: Friendship Press, 1955, p. 26. Used by permission.

native land, but we have not lost our self-dignity and hope that somewhere in the world a place will be found for us where we will no longer be obliged to live in camps and receive charity. All we want is to have a chance to start a new decent life under democratic conditions.

Along with the hungry and the homeless are the helpless including, according to United Nations estimate, 60,000,000 children in need; the hospital-less, numbering millions who are without medical care; the hurt, who have suffered in major disasters; the haunted, who are beset by superstition, fear, and ignorance; and the hopeless, whom no one can number, for whom life's burdens have been so many, so heavy, and so constant that hope at last has given way to despair. For all of these the Christian with a sense of world responsibility will be concerned to do any possible deeds of compassion, and fortunately through the church and its agencies direct action toward the alleviation of such needs as have been mentioned is possible.

Commission

The Christian has a world responsibility not only because his participation in the spirit of Christ leads him to compassion for the needy everywhere, but also because he is under a commission which encompasses the world. It is concerning the area where the seed of the kingdom is to be sown that it is said: "The field is the world." "Go therefore and make disciples of all nations," is the command of Christ to his disciples as they understood his final imperative to them. The words of the present book are being written in a place where one's window frames the Golden Gate of San Francisco Bay. The Golden Gate stands for adventure, for voyages have been launched from here to all the seven seas. Yet of all adventures there has surely been none greater than that of the Christian world mission. There is beauty at the Golden Gate, for this is the entrance to one of the world's most spectacular harbors. But directly in line with the Gate is Alcatraz Island, the site of a federal prison. Thus even amidst beauty the shadow of human failure appears, and we are reminded of our need throughout all the world of that greater beauty which is the glory of God. The Golden Gate also stands for commerce since, from the days of the Gold Rush on, it has witnessed the entry and departure of a great volume of commercial shipping. But what commerce is so richly rewarding as the commerce of Christian missions? Schools, hospitals, food, and faith—these have been our most valuable exports, and these are chiefly what have built up such a "reservoir of good will" as we continue to have throughout the world. But there is danger also at the Golden Gate, the danger of powerful currents, rushing tides, and sudden fogs, and more than one vessel has come to grief there. There is danger out in the world too, the danger of the conflict of ideologies and the strife of peoples, but from the time when Jesus "set his face to go to Jerusalem" despite the danger which awaited him there, his followers have had courage to dare peril in his service. Yet again the Golden Gate carries a suggestion of eternity. From many viewpoints the great San Francisco Bay appears to be land-locked, but out there where the headlands seem to meet, the Golden Gate opens to the almost boundless ocean. Life, too, may look like a landlocked harbor, but where the outline of the shore seems to meet in death, Christian faith speaks of a gateway which opens to the ocean of eternity, and the Christian world mission makes known everywhere the message of everlasting life. Thus we may spell out something of the symbolic significance of one gateway to the world, but whatever window a Christian looks out of will be to him a window upon the world and a reminder of the commission to go into all the world with the gospel.

Contribution

Finally, by deeds of compassion and by obedience to the commission of Christ, his follower may make contribution to the unity and peace of the world. Peace can scarcely abide in a world where men remain hungry, homeless, and hurt. The attack upon these problems is fundamental to the establishing of a more secure order of society. Yet even more fundamental is the making known of the message of God's love which gives human life its meaning, and of Christ's way in which men may at last realize their brotherhood in all the earth.

CHAPTER 14

Diagnosing the Sickness of the World[1]

The Christian has a responsibility in relation to the whole world. This has been evident ever since the parable of Jesus taught that "the field is the world," and it is a fact which it is only the more necessary to emphasize in the present nuclear-space age, an age in which atomic power can either destroy or benefit all people, and in which the swift circling of the earth by artificial satellites adds another dramatic demonstration of how inescapably bound together all people are. The preceding chapter has stated this responsibility in its broad terms and suggested that the practical good deeds and the proclaimed message of the Christian world mission are of fundamental importance for the unity and peace of the world. The present chapter is intended to analyze the problem of world peace and unity somewhat further, and to show something more of the directions indicated by Christian thought in which the solution of the problem is to be

[1] This chapter appeared originally in *The Christian Century*, LXVIII, 39, Sept. 26, 1951, pp. 1098-1099, and is reproduced here with adaptations. Copyright 1951 Christian Century Foundation. Reprinted by permission.

sought. In order to do this we may speak of the problem of the world in terms of sickness, an idea which is not new and not confined to religious thought. A biblical seer spoke of the tree whose leaves would be for the healing of nations, and a modern cartoonist pictures the globe swathed in bandages. But what is the nature of the sickness? We must know this before we can hope to prescribe for a cure.

Diagnosis

A first item in a diagnosis of the sickness of the world was suggested by a remark of Douglas Steere when he mentioned "our mental hardening of the categories."[2] A category is a grouping. When a grouping is made it is very easy for its outlines to become exceedingly hard and fast. A few years ago the category "German" signified only what was undesirable. Therefore study of the German language was dropped from many schools, though a considerable part of the scientific and other literature of the world is written in it. During the First World War the playing of German music was banned from the concert stage, though the compositions of Bach and Wagner are surely frontierless.

The category "Russian" went swiftly from one extreme to the other. Signifying herioc endurance when Russian armies were aligned with ours in a world war, it has more recently bid fair to eclipse anything ever signified in connotation of evil by "German." A reverse metamorphosis has probably taken place with regard to Spain. Until recently synonymous with fascism, when the land began to provide us with naval and air bases "Spain" began to stand for something good rather than bad. "Jew" and "Roman Catholic" and "Negro" are other categories that harden swiftly. Such hardening of the categories works to prevent straight thinking and is part of the sickness of the world.

[2] In *The Christian Century*, May 16, 1951, p. 610.

The world is also suffering from chronic inflammation of the relationships. The national states, which are the characteristic form of organization in the modern world, rub against each other producing friction at the point of contact. One cannot travel more than a few hours in Europe without coming to a national boundary. There customs must be passed, a whole barricade of regulations surmounted, money exchanged, and a new language employed. Guns face each other across the borders. Such frictions exist throughout the world. That the inflammation at these points of relationship is chronic is indicated by the fact that since 1861 there has not been a single year when there was no war going on somewhere in the world.

Furthermore, the world is afflicted with hypertrophy of the material. Hypertrophy is a state of overgrowth or excessive development, which may arise from excessive use or attempted compensation for a deficiency. The development of material things in the world is clearly out of proportion to the rest of human life. Thomas A. Edison noted this and said: "If there is a God he will not let us advance much further materially until we catch up spiritually." E. E. Slosson declared: "In our civilization the mechanical forces have got ahead of the moral forces. Man is mounted upon a bigger horse than he can ride." Omar N. Bradley said: "Ours is a world of nuclear giants and ethical infants."

Continuing the diagnosis, we find the world to be suffering from pernicious anonymity of the masses. Everywhere on earth when one becomes acquainted with the common man one finds him about like the ordinary person anywhere else. He does not want war; he does want a chance to live peacefully and decently. An observer back from eleven months in forty-eight countries on both sides of three areas of tension (Communist and western Europe, Arab and Jewish Palestine, Pakistan and India) says: "Everywhere we sensed a universal hunger for peace." The ordinary man in America today is certainly not the imperialist that Asiatic propaganda makes him out to be. He too just wants the chance for a decent life. But unfortunately these common people of all the countries remain largely anonymous to one another. Often they are ineffectual in making what they want known even to their own governments. In the United States of America only 51.5 per cent of the civilians of voting age voted in the presidential election in 1948; 62.7 per cent in 1952; and 60.4 per cent in 1956.[3] Thus the anonymity and ineffectiveness of the masses of people are a pernicious fact in the world's sickness.

Prescription

Turning from diagnosis to prescription, one would suggest for the patient, first, therapeutic doses, weekly or oftener, of the gospel of human brotherhood. This is the most potent solvent available for the hardening of the categories. Speaking of how to attack the caste system, which is one form in which categories harden, a recent writer declares that belief in the fatherhood of God and its necessary corollary, the brotherhood of man, is "our greatest affirmative religious resource."

Next one would prescribe membership and exercise in the organization of the United Nations. Judicious exercise in a gymnasium or elsewhere can conduce to the healthy functioning of the joints in the human body. By exercising ourselves constantly and patiently in the United Nations we may hope to get our international relationships out of an inflamed state into a more healthy condition.

Again, we need a compensatory development of the ethical and spiritual to offset the hypertrophy of the material.

[3] *Statistical Abstract of the U.S. 1957* (U.S. Department of Commerce, Bureau of the Census), p. 350.

That this is not an entirely visionary part of the prescription is indicated by the fact that in our time a multi-million-dollar foundation has taken as its areas of concern (1) world peace; (2) freedom and democracy; (3) the well-being of people everywhere; (4) educational advance in civic and spiritual areas; and (5) application of science to human welfare.

Also, an increase in acquaintance and a release of energies among all the common people of the world are necessary. In a remarkable article in *Foreign Affairs*, George F. Kennan described the people of Russia in these words:

> They are a people whose progress out of darkness and squalor has been a painful one, marked by enormous sufferings and punctuated by heart-rending setbacks. Nowhere on the face of the globe has the tinny flame of faith in the dignity and charity of man flickered more precariously under the winds that tore at it. Yet it has never gone out; it is not extinguished today even in the heart of the Russian land; and whoever studies the struggle of the Russian spirit through the ages can only bare his head in admiration before those Russian people who kept it alight through their sacrifices and sufferings. Then he drew this conclusion: It would be tragic if our indignation over Soviet outlooks and policies led us to make ourselves the accomplices of Russian despotism by forgetting the greatness of the Russian people, losing our confidence in their genius and their potential for good, and placing ourselves in opposition to their national feelings. The vital importance of this becomes even clearer when we reflect that we in the outside world who believe in the cause of freedom will never prevail in any struggle against the destructive workings of Soviet power unless the Russian people are our willing allies.[4]

Assurance

A physician's work is not done until he has given some word of assurance to his patient. At the commencement exercises of students graduating in a field of healing, I heard the motto quoted: "To heal sometimes, to relieve often, to comfort always." Sometimes it is the comfort and assurance the doctor gives that, as much as anything else, make the healing forces effective.

Some assurance may be derived from the fact that our patient has been sick and has gotten well before. More than once the world has reached such a crisis that the faint-hearted have abandoned all hope; but contrary to expectations, a revival of health has come.

There are also many white corpuscles in the world's bloodstream today. When disease attacks the body, it is the white corpuscles that rush to repel the invading germs. At a time when much of Europe was torn by war, Allan A. Hunter described the work of certain men and women of good will under this very figure of speech. Of the "white corpuscles in Europe" he said: "Rallying to those places where the wounds are most dangerous are reconciling forces. Patiently they are removing the poisonous matter. Secretly they are making it possible for the broken tissues to be restored."[5] Christians ought to be like that everywhere, and it is heartening to know that there are more such potential white corpuscles in the bloodstream of the world than ever before.

Finally, there is assurance in the fact that the gospel which has healed individuals can also be expected to heal society. This was the confident expectation of the one who wrote about the tree of life which he saw in his vision: "And the leaves of the tree were for the healing of the nations."

[5] *White Corpuscles in Europe* (Chicago and New York: Willett, Clark and Company, 1939), p. ix.

CHAPTER 15

Pain and Progress[1]

In the preceding chapter we spoke metaphorically of the sickness of the world, and in an earlier chapter we noted the statement of Paul that "the whole creation has been groaning in travail together until now." It is the purpose of the present chapter to explore further the relationship of the fact of pain to the movement of the world toward the kingdom of God, a kingdom in which at last, according to biblical hope, there shall not be "pain any more."

Suffering Pains

Charles H. Brent, first missionary bishop of the Philippines, once said, "The world's work has always been done by men who have suffered pains or taken pains." *Does* the suffering of pains go along with the doing of the world's work? In general, several books of our time have converged toward an affirmative answer. In *A Study of History*, Arnold J. Toynbee remarks that the popular supposition is that civilization develops when an endowed people is situated in a favorable environment, but himself defends the opposite thesis, namely, that civilization emerges when a people re-

[1] This chapter appeared originally in *The Pulpit*, XIX, 10, Oct. 1948, pp. 224-226, and is reproduced here with adaptations. Copyrighted by the Christian Century Foundation and reprinted by permission of *The Pulpit* from the issue of October, 1948.

sponds to a situation of special challenge. Hard country, new ground, blows, pressures, and penalizations are the sort of thing in response to which great achievements have been made in the development of civilization. In a sociological study entitled, *Man and Society in Calamity*, Pitirim A. Sorokin declares that the great calamities of history are not an unmixed evil. Along with the destruction and damage that they do, they have their constructive effects, and are indeed the "great educators of mankind." Likewise in a survey of religious development extending *From the Stone Age to Christianity*, William F. Albright has said that "real spiritual progress can be achieved only through catastrophe and suffering," and has pointed out that this progress reaches new levels after the "profound catharsis which accompanies major upheavals."

The same thing that is observed in the history of the world is also often true in individual lives. Only through the suffering of pains do we make progress. Certainly many a forward step in human achievement, such as the exploration of the polar regions, the crossing of the oceans, and the pioneering of the air, has been taken only because individuals were willing to risk and often to suffer pains. Furthermore, pain seems many times to be a necessary stimulus and a driving force. Emerson said: "Whilst man sits on the cushion of advantages, he goes to sleep. When he is pushed, tormented, defeated, he has a chance to learn something; he has been put on his wits, on his manhood; he has gained facts; learns his ignorance; is cured of the insanity of conceit; has got moderation and real skill." Not only this, but it is in the very depths of suffering that some of man's creative insights have come to him. Thus it was that Tchaikowsky in his fifties was driven to declare, "My faith in myself is terribly shattered, and it seems to me that my role has ended," but one week later began work on the greatest symphony he ever wrote, the *Pathétique*.

We are able then to concur in the first part of the observation of Bishop Brent, that the world's work has always
been done by men who have suffered pains. Our second
question concerns the second part of his statement. Has the
work of the world always been done by men who have taken
pains?

Taking Pains

To this we would no doubt be quite readily inclined to
assent, except for the thought that perhaps some great
achievements have been the result of insight, intuition, and
genius rather than of painstaking labor. Let us note a few
actual examples, and see what the true situation has been.

In the field of science, the discovery of insulin was an
event of the greatest importance. This was accomplished
by Frederick Grant Banting, a young Canadian surgeon.
His practice was so poor that he had to teach to eke out a
living, and on one particular evening was poring over his
lecture notes for the next day. The subject was diabetes,
the dread disease about which as yet so little was known.
He read conflicting theories, case histories, accounts of experiments with dogs, until his head was awhirl and at last
he went wearily to bed. At two o'clock in the morning he
got up, turned on a light, and wrote these three sentences
in his notebook: "Tie off pancreatic duct of dogs. Wait six
to eight weeks for degeneration. Remove residue and ex-
tract." It was those three sentences which led to the discovery of insulin. And how had they come to be written?
As an intuition bursting upon the mind of a man in the
middle of the night? Yes—but only after the most laborious
efforts had been made to master all relevant data could
the creative synthesis flash clear.

In music, perhaps most of all, the requirement would
seem to be for talent and genius. Yet if one admires the
great and apparently instinctive mastery exhibited by a

Paderewski, one must remember that that artist himself declared, "Before I was a master, I was a slave." Yet again, in literature surely some have a veritable gift of writing. Nevertheless, Jean Jacques Rousseau said, "My manuscripts, blotted, scratched, interlined, and scarcely legible, attest the trouble they cost me"; and Montesquieu, upon completing *The Spirit of Laws,* a work that influenced the framing of the Constitution of the United States of America, told friends, "You will read this treatise in a few hours, yet the labor expended on it has whitened my hair." Truly, "genius is the capacity for taking infinite pains."

Conquering Pain

If it is indeed true that the world's work has been done by men who have suffered pains or taken pains, let us advance to ask yet a third question: Is there any connection between the two things, the suffering of pains and the taking of pains? Sometimes, at least, there is. Sometimes, by taking pains men enter into a fellowship with those who suffer pains, and together a forward step is taken toward the conquering of pain. We do not, for the most part, choose whether or not we will suffer pains. As in the case of Job, pain often falls upon men irrespective of choice or merit. But we do choose whether or not we will take pains. Some people, as a matter of fact, seem to spend most of their lives trying to avoid taking pains about anything. But others choose to take pains. They take pains with their studies, with their preparation, and with their life work all the way through. And sometimes such taking of pains brings them into relationship with those who suffer pains, and together some new bit of conquest of pain is accomplished.

Here, in brief outline, is how this has worked out in one particular area. The area is that of pain in the medical and surgical sense, and the story can be read in its full detail

in René Fülöp-Miller's book called *Triumph Over Pain*.[2]
The written record of pain is as ancient as the cuneiform
tablet which preserves the inscription of a Babylonian king's
daughter: "Pain has seized my body. May God tear this
pain out." From then until now the cry of pain has gone
up. Some have said it could not be otherwise. Does not
Genesis declare that man must live in labor and pain? Surgery was developed, however, which in many cases could
help; yet in the old days it was itself an occasion of such
fright and pain that the cure was often worse than the
disease. And again many said that this could not be otherwise. Dr. Alfred Velpeau, a famous French surgeon, declared: "The abolishment of pain in surgery is a chimera.
It is absurd to go on seeking it today. *Knife* and *pain* are
two words in surgery that must forever be associated in the
consciousness of the patient."

Other men, meanwhile, were taking pains to learn and
know. Joseph Priestley was one of these. He was a minister
in England and he lived near a brewery. In the Providence
of God something good came out of something evil. Priestley visited the brewery and watched the little bubbles of
air which rose to the surface of the fermenting liquid. Every
brewer was familiar with the phenomenon and thought no
more about it. Priestley, driven by an insatiable scientific
curiosity and by a profound religious faith which regarded
all natural phenomena as manifestations of the glory of God,
studied and experimented and discovered oxygen, and later
nitrous oxide as well. Then the story goes on with Humphry
Davy, a young man who ventured to inhale the nitrous
oxide and discovered the strange properties because of
which it became known as laughing gas. At this point
Michael Faraday entered the picture, making a memorandum to the effect that vapor of ether mixed with air might
be inhaled to produce effects similar to those of nitrous

[2] New York: The Literary Guild of America, Inc., 1938.

oxide. This memorandum became the basis of anesthesia with ether, but it was another painstaking worker who made the actual application.

William Thomas Green Morton, a young dentist in Boston, was distressed by the pain he had to cause his patients, and experimented with ether until with its help he performed an extraction without pain. When he proposed the use of the same method for surgical operations, there was general skepticism, since most of the learned and famous doctors shared the opinion of Dr. Velpeau that surgery and pain would always be inseparable. But Dr. Warren of the Massachusetts General Hospital agreed to a trial. With Morton administering the ether, an operation was successfully performed, the patient for the first time in all the history of the world sleeping peacefully the entire time. When, at the close, Dr. Warren turned to the crowded amphitheater of the operating room and exclaimed, "Gentlemen, this is no humbug," great applause broke out. That was on October 16, 1846, only a little over one hundred years ago, and a major forward step was taken in the conquest of pain. How had it come about? By the suffering of pains on the part of untold numbers of people which served as an ever more insistent summons, and by the taking of pains to learn and know and do on the part of a series of brave men. Both together, the sufferers of pains and the takers of pains, wrought out a triumph over pain.

Now this story, a highly condensed account of what has actually happened in one area, is also a symbol and a suggestion of what may happen in many other areas. Unconquered diseases, iniquitous social stratifications, war and crime, all these things and many more still bring the suffering of pains to multitudes of people. From their very sufferings the summons arises. It is a call to other men to take pains, by voluntary choice, to bring triumph over pains in these areas too.

CHAPTER 16

The Impossible Possibility of Christian Ethics

The Christian imperative in such a world as ours, a few of the outlines of which have been discussed in the immediately preceding chapters, does not call men to easy tasks. In fact in such a world as this the Christian ethic has every appearance of impossibility. We may find an accurate statement of the situation in Luke 18:27—" 'What is impossible with men is possible with God' "—and in this text the first word emphasized is "impossible."

Impossible

The teachings of Jesus seem to be impossibly difficult. He himself said that they were very hard. A man came up to him and asked what he must do to have eternal life. Jesus cited the Ten Commandments, and the man said that he had kept them from his youth. Then Jesus asked him to sell his goods, distribute to the poor, and come and follow him. Thereupon the man went away sad because he had many possessions, and Jesus said to his disciples: " 'How hard it will be for those who have riches to enter the kingdom of God!'" (Mark 10:23.) After that, in the record of this event in the Gospel according to Mark, there is a sentence which is reported differently in different manuscripts. The later manuscripts record that Jesus said, "Children, how hard it is for those who trust in riches to enter the kingdom of God!" (Mark 10:24 margin.) This makes his statement simply a reiteration of what he has already said. But the oldest manuscripts, Codex Vaticanus and Codex Sinaiticus, do not contain the words about trusting in riches, and the sentence reads, "Children, how hard it is to enter the kingdom of God." This is presumably the more correct report of the words of Jesus, and it means that he said flatly and as a general statement that it is hard to enter the kingdom. Then he returned to the case of the man with great possessions and in the light of what had happened remarked, "It is easier for a camel to go through the eye of a needle than for a rich man to enter the kingdom of God." A camel is an ungainly beast, with long neck and sprawling legs. The eye of a needle is what some of us cannot even put a thread through. This is such a hard saying that commentators have endeavored to soften it. Some have pointed to a gate at Jerusalem which contains a smaller door. The smaller door might be the eye of the needle, through which a camel could barely squeeze if he scraped off all his baggage. Others have noted the similarity in Greek between the word for camel and the word for rope, and have supposed that the original saying spoke of a rope going through the eye of a needle. But on other occasions also Jesus spoke in hyperbole, and it is probable that he uttered this saying in the form in which we have it and with the meaning we naturally attach to it. Entrance into the kingdom of God is so hard that it may be illustrated by what is palpable absurdity and utter impossibility.

The disciples thought that what Jesus taught was too hard

to be done. After his statement about the camel and the eye of the needle, they asked in astonishment, "Then who can be saved?" They evidently thought that demands such as he was making could not be fulfilled. If this was what was required for salvation, one might as well give up hope. On another occasion Jesus gave teaching concerning marriage and divorce, and as the disciples listen, one can almost see them shaking their heads sadly. " 'If such is the case of a man with his wife,' " they say, " 'it is not expedient to marry.' " (Matthew 19:10.) If it is necessary to follow such teachings as these, they think, it is better not to get into the situation where they apply.

It is also possible to demonstrate by our own logical analysis that the teachings of Jesus are difficult to the point of impossibility. Consider the possible implications of the two incidents just cited from the Gospels. In one case Jesus asked a man to give up his possessions; in the other case the disciples concluded that abstinence from marriage was indicated. But if poverty and celibacy were applied universally, society would be destroyed; and if these principles are taken as applicable to only a limited number, two sets of standards are the result, the harder to be followed by the more perfect, the easier to be accepted by the less perfect.

Consider also the tremendous inwardness of the requirements of Jesus. When he conversed with the man with the great possessions, he first of all mentioned to him the Ten Commandments, actually citing five or six of them, "Do not kill, Do not commit adultery, Do not steal," and so on, and the man affirmed that he had kept all these. Here at least ethics was on the level of possibility. A man could honestly say that he had kept these commandments and had not done what they forbade. But supposing that man had been present on the day Jesus gave the teachings contained in the Sermon on the Mount, could he still have declared that he had kept

the commandments? Consider a single one of the commandments and see what, according to the Sermon on the Mount,
Jesus considered it to require. "You have heard that it was
said," quoted Jesus, " 'You shall not kill.' " That is one of the
ethical injunctions of the Ten Commandments, and Jesus
adds the statement of the customary result of an infraction:
"and whoever kills shall be liable to judgment." Then he
proceeds to state his own exposition of the meaning of this
commandment. This is done in a threefold statement, each
part of which is presumably intended to say the same thing
in a slightly variant form for the sake of emphasis, a manner
of composition characteristic of Semitic style. The first part of
the statement initiates the contrast of the teaching of Jesus
with the commandment of old: "But I say to you that every
one who is angry with his brother shall be liable to judgment." This is the inwardness of the requirement of Jesus.
Anger as well as murder renders liable to judgment. The
second part of the statement continues: "Whoever insults his
brother shall be liable to the council." The expression rendered "insults" in the Revised Standard Version, is literally to
say *Raca*, as may be seen in the American Standard Version,
and this is presumably an obscure Aramaic word of contempt.
The council is one of the local courts which administered
justice among the Jews. The third part of the statement is:
"and whoever says, 'You fool!' shall be liable to the hell of
fire." Here we have the vocative of the Greek adjective
mōros, a word which means stupid or foolish. The neuter of
this word is *mōron*, and one does not even have to know
Greek to recognize that this is the direct source of a word
well known in the English language. Jesus has, therefore,
declared that whoever calls someone else a moron is liable
to punishment. So, if someone almost collides with you in
traffic and you utter an ancient biblical word of abuse, or if
someone does something stupid and you say, "You moron!"

you have been angry with your brother and, since anger is as much prohibited by the saying of Jesus as is murder, you have broken the commandment and lost the way which leads to life. In succeeding paragraphs in the Sermon on the Mount the same carrying back of the import of the commandment from the external act to the internal motive is applied to other requirements of the law. Who, then, can hope to live up to this incisively inward demand of the ethic of Jesus?

Note also what we may call the intensity of the requirement of Jesus. He says: "You . . . must be perfect, as your heavenly Father is perfect." (Matthew 5:48.) Since God must be considered to be utterly perfect, this seems like a call to attain to a standard which is surely above the reach of human attainment. Does not Jesus himself elsewhere say: "No one is good but God alone"? (Mark 10:18.)

Possible

Yet the teachings of Jesus must be possible. He gave them, so he must have meant them. Often they are in the imperative: do, do not, go, come, sell, buy, give. Usually they are in the present: therefore he could hardly have meant that they were only something to be done at some time far distant in the future. The disciples, moreover, took the teachings seriously. They may have shaken their heads about them sometimes and wondered how anybody could ever hope to perform them, nevertheless they remembered what Jesus said. They taught what he had said to others. They wrote down his sayings, and we think that a collection of the sayings of Jesus is a fundamental source of our present Gospel records.

We may also maintain that the teachings of Jesus do not actually point to the destruction of society, as by some interpretations they may appear to do, but rather to the transformation of society. The teaching of Jesus does not in fact require all people to give up all possessions. This he asked of one particular rich man. But as far as the record shows, he did not ask it of Zacchaeus, for example, who was evidently also a man of wealth. He did expect Zacchaeus to deal honorably, and in the presence of Jesus, Zacchaeus himself was moved to determine upon restitution for wrongs he had done. Not only in regard to wealth but also marriage and other topics which Jesus touched upon, his teachings would appear, properly understood, to work not to destroy but to transform for good man's relationships. Taken simply and seriously, they have indeed often done that and, if our faith were only sufficient, they would doubtless even far more often be effective in this way. Seeking to find the way to apply the teachings of Jesus to contemporary life, Charles M. Sheldon used to approach problems by saying, "If Christ were here on earth again. . . . If Jesus were invited into any pulpit in America today. . . . I cannot imagine Christ keeping silent on this matter." At Paris, Georges Clemenceau sneered about Woodrow Wilson, "He spoke like Jesus Christ." Gerald Heard remarked, "Ah, if he only *had!*" It was indeed in application of fundamental principles of Christ that Wilson pleaded for the League of Nations, and that organization, imperfect as it was, prepared the way for the United Nations, today our last best hope. Halford E. Luccock remarks, "We can see more clearly than ever before in history that it is not Jesus who is a sentimentalist";[1] and Francis B. Sayre writes:

Christ is often pictured as an impractical dreamer, an idealist ignorant of the cold realities of this workaday world. That is profoundly untrue. He was the most downright and practical realist the world has ever known. Nineteen centuries of human experience have proved that lives and institutions built on his teachings bear infinite

[1] Stuber and Clark, eds., *op. cit.*, p. 91. Used by permission of Halford E. Luccock.

fruit and that those built on an opposing philosophy prove ultimately self-defeating, and perish.[2]

Possible and Impossible

The teachings of Jesus appear to be impossible, yet they must be possible. As a matter of fact it is just because there is something both of impossibility and of possibility about them that they are so great. It is in this paradoxical fact that much of the challenge of his teachings lies. If what he tells us to do were utterly and only impossible, we would be discouraged. If what he tells us to do were quite possible, then we would not be interested. The nature of such challenge may be illustrated in the field of science where so many things once believed and even theoretically proved impossible have become actual. Books were written to prove that man could not fly, but man flies. One research scholar says, "The word 'impossible' is to a scientist much like a spur to a horse." In a research laboratory is the slogan, "The difficult can be done quickly, the impossible will take a little longer." The teachings of Jesus may be called ideals, and someone says of them: "Ideals are like the stars—we never reach them, but like the mariners on the sea, we chart our course by them." The teachings are the principles of the kingdom of God. As the principles of heaven they will necessarily look impossible upon earth, yet nothing less than these principles will ultimately work right. Emil Brunner says: "Only the impossible is worthy to be obeyed. For only the impossible is the Will of God."[3] And Robert J. McCracken writes:

Scrap the ethics of the Sermon on the Mount for the power politics of the superman or the super-state, try to build peace on the basis of superior force, not superior justice—that spells the defeat of all our

[2] *Ibid.* Used by permission of Francis B. Sayre.
[3] From *The Mediator* (p. 419) by Emil Brunner. Copyright 1947, by W. L. Jenkins, The Westminster Press. Used by permission.

hopes and brings doom in the end. Somehow everything we do that is cruel and combative and selfish sooner or later breaks down in personal life, business life, national and international life. It doesn't last. It won't work. Selfishness is the root principle of all neuroticism. No way works well in God's world but the morally right way. About this Christ is both right and relevant. He affirms the reality of love in the face of the reality of power. Love, he says, is the groundwork of the universe, the ultimate meaning of life.[4]

It is because the teachings of Jesus are at once possible and impossible that we are kept humble. We fail to do them, yet we know we ought to do them. Willard L. Sperry has written:

The demands of Christianity are absolute; that is their strength. Human nature being what it is there must be, therefore, a contrast between profession and practice. Even at the cost of this painful and humiliating discrepancy there is everything to be said for maintaining in theory the absolute and arbitrary requirements of Christian faith and Christian ethics. It is only when we cease to feel and be troubled by the discrepancy that we lapse into hypocrisy.[5]

Likewise Emil Brunner has said, "The man who calls this ethic impracticable has understood it far better than the man who speaks easily about its beautiful inwardness and simplicity."[6]

And yet again it is precisely because the teachings of Jesus are both possible and impossible that we are turned to God. This, in fact, was the outcome of the matter in the conversation of Jesus with his disciples following upon the incident of the man with great possessions which we cited at the beginning of this chapter. When the disciples deemed what Jesus had said very hard, and asked despairingly, "Then who can be saved?" Jesus replied, according to Mark 10:27, "With men it is impossible, but not with

---

[4] In *The Pulpit*, Jan. 1957, p. 21. Copyrighted by the Christian Century Foundation and reprinted by permission of *The Pulpit* from the issue of January, 1957.

[5] Stuber and Clark, eds., *op. cit.*, p. 120.

[6] Brunner, *op. cit.*

God; for all things are possible with God," or according to
the more concise version in Luke 18:27. "What is impossible
with men is possible with God." The teaching of Jesus
turns us to God, and it is only by his redeeming help that
the things of which Jesus speaks come to pass in our lives.
R. W. Barbour says, "God does all before He asks us to do
anything; He redeems before He enjoins; and only the re-
deemed can truly keep His commandments";[7] and D. T.
Niles writes, "The Sermon on the Mount is more a statement
of what will happen to a man when he allows Jesus to get
hold of him, than a statement of what a man must do if he is
to follow Jesus."[8]

Putting the paradox with which we have been dealing in
terms of the apprehension of perfection and the awareness of
imperfection, Reinhold Niebuhr writes:

All men who live with any degree of serenity live by some assurance of grace. In every life there must at least be times and seasons
when the good is felt as a present possession and not as a far-off goal.
The sinner must feel himself 'justified,' that is, he must feel that his
imperfections are understood and sympathetically appreciated as well
as challenged. Whenever he finds himself in a circle of love where he
is 'completely known and all forgiven' something of the mercy of
God is revealed to him and he catches a glimpse of the very perfection
which has eluded him. Perhaps the most sublime insight of Jewish
prophets and the Christian gospel is the knowledge that since perfection is love, the apprehension of perfection is at once the means
of seeing one's imperfection and the consoling assurance of grace
which makes this realization bearable. This ultimate paradox of high
religion is not an invention of theologians or priests. It is constantly
validated by the most searching experiences of life.[9]

Of such nature is the ethic of the kingdom of God. It is
both presently relevant and also endlessly challenging. It is

[7] *Thoughts,* p. 100. Quoted by Baillie, *op. cit.,* 187.

[8] *That They May Have Life,* p. 47. Used by permission of Harper
& Brothers, publishers.

[9] *Reflections on the End of an Era* (New York: Charles Scribner's
Sons, 1934), pp. 284-285. Used by permission.

so radical that it belongs to the final consummation in which the kingdom will be fully established, yet it is a way of life which has already appeared as a reality in Jesus as the Christ and is, at least in some wise, shared in by his followers. It is the way of the new age of God, the new age in which, even even in the age of atomic power and space travel, lies our ultimate hope.